ESSAYS AND STUDIES
1975

BEING VOLUME TWENTY-EIGHT OF THE NEW SERIES
OF ESSAYS AND STUDIES COLLECTED FOR
THE ENGLISH ASSOCIATION

BY ROBERT ELLRODT

JOHN MURRAY

FIFTY ALBEMARLE STREET LONDON

Printed in Great Britain by
Cox & Wyman Ltd, London, Fakenham and Reading
0 7195 3232 9

Contents

Foreword

When the English Association honoured me with an invitation to collect essays for this volume it was suggested I should approach Continental as well as English scholars. There were fewer clouds over the political future of Europe at that time, but why should they concern us? Unmindful of the statesman's fair or foul weather, University men and women have long laboured hard in the field of English studies for the common market of European culture.

The array of Professors in the list of contributors is not the mark of French academic prejudice. Rightly or wrongly I thought that the Continental authors of works already well known in England would be more 'representative' than younger scholars, however brilliant, for the celebration of the long-standing links between the Universities of Great Britain, Germany, Italy and Belgium. The special request for an essay on Shelley, unjustly neglected for many years in *Essays and Studies*, proved, however, an opportunity for introducing a French representative of the younger generation of critics. Limitations of space alone prevented my inviting contributions from Dutch and Scandinavian scholars, whose services to English literature are so widely known and valued.

To preserve a proper balance the volume also includes essays by eminent English scholars. Special thanks are due to them for obliging us with their contributions on this particular occasion.

The absence of mediaeval studies in this European volume might seem to imply a disregard of our common inheritance. This was not intended. At the last moment Professor Wickham for various reasons had to shift his interest from Mediaeval to Shakespearean drama. Who could regret it after reading his fascinating interpretation of *The Tempest*?

Robert Ellrodt
University of Nice

I

Masque and Anti-masque in 'The Tempest'

GLYNNE WICKHAM

MANY critics, sensing instinctively that some connection exists between Jacobean Court Masques and Shakespeare's later plays, have drawn attention to it; but few of them have chosen to pursue this intuitive recognition to the point of regarding that connection as likely to reside in anything more substantial than Court spectacle grounded in painting, carpentry, machines, and the exquisite costume designs of Inigo Jones. They have therefore been content, in general, to confine comment to the spectacular quality of the later plays—notably the tragi-comedies—and to leave it at that.

In recent years, however, several critics (Muriel Bradbrook, Inga-Stina Ewbank, Emrys Jones, Roy Strong and Stephen Orgel among them) have taken the matter much further and have given Ben Jonson the credit for knowing what he was saying when describing masques as 'spectacles of state' and 'Court hieroglyphics'; and, in choosing to regard masques as riddles that audiences were expected to solve by intelligent interpretation of the visual and verbal iconography, they have followed the track pioneered some thirty years ago by Donald Gordon in his monographs on *The Hue and Cry After Cupid* (1608) and *Hymenaei* (1606).[1] As a result a much clearer understanding is now emerging of the relationship between masque and anti-masque; of masques as ornaments to state occasions that sought to contrast sense with understanding, order with disorder, a stable society subject to a God-like monarch with an anarchic world of bestiality and folly; of the direct analogies and indirect associations between the persons and behaviour

[1] See D. J. Gordon, '*Hymenaei*'; *Ben Jonson's Masque of Union*, Journal of the Warburg and Courtauld Institute, viii 1945, and 'Ben Jonson's Haddington Masque', M.L.R. XLII, 2, (April, 1947).

of characters and performers in masques on the one hand, and the individuals in Jacobean Court society on the other hand who commissioned the masques, paid for them, and either acted in them or struggled for precedence in obtaining seats to watch them. A no less important service has been accomplished for the musical and choreographic elements of masque by Andrew Sabol which helps to reinforce this clearer understanding of the nature and purpose of these costly spectacles.[1]

At last, therefore, it is becoming possible to replace vague, critical generalizations about the connections between masque as a dramatic genre and stage-plays of the Jacobean and Caroline era— with a more precise commentary on the specific links between some masques and particular stage-plays. Those now accepted between *Hymenaei* and *The Maid's Tragedy,* between *Macbeth* and *The Masque of Queens,* and between *The Masque of Oberon* and *The Winter's Tale* may serve here as examples. Beyond them I have myself, in two recent articles, ventured to draw more extensive parallels between the political and philosophical implications of certain masques devised by Samuel Daniel and Ben Jonson and Shakespearean tragi-comedy.[2]

Of all such links, however, the most obvious and yet the most neglected in terms of serious critical analysis is that 'variety of his art' which Prospero tells Ariel he must 'bestow upon the eyes' of Ferdinand and Miranda in *The Tempest* (IV. i. 40).

In directing this play for the National Theatre recently Peter Hall abruptly reversed all that, and seized upon this aspect of the play as the element that was to determine the whole spirit and style of his production. The 'masque' was indeed spectacular, with a singing Iris in baroque attire descending on a brilliantly illumi-

[1] See Andrew Sabol, *Songs and Dances for the Stuart Masque*, Brown University Press, Providence, Rhode Island, 1959, and 'New documents on Shirley's masque *The Triumph of Peace*', *Music and Letters*, Vol. 47, No. 1, Jan. 1966, 10–26.

[2] See G. Wickham, 'From Tragedy to Tragi-Comedy: *King Lear* as Prologue', *Shakespeare Survey* 26, 1973, 33–48, and 'Romance and Emblem: A Study, in the Dramatic Structure of *The Winter's Tale*', *The Elizabethan Theatre III*, ed. David Galloway, Macmillan, 1973, 82–99. See also 'To fly or not to fly? The problem of Hecate in Shakespeare's *Macbeth*', *Essays on Drama and Theatre: Liber Amicorum Benjamin Hunningher*, Moussault, Amsterdam, 1973, 171–82.

nated rainbow to summon a no less voluptuously dressed Ceres (a counter-tenor at that) for the entertainment of a Juno throned in peacock feathers floating on a cloud machine and disguised, as it appeared, to resemble Queen Elizabeth I, complete with far-thingale, lace collar and red hair.

In one respect at least this treatment proved unquestionably correct, since it restored to this 'masque' its due pre-eminence as the theatrical climax of the whole play. And yet, in another and more important respect it was no less self-evidently wrong since it soon became apparent that the iconography chosen by the designer, John Berry, was both haphazardly applied and largely incorrect. Thus this expensively prepared climax, by failing to reveal—or unmask—the moral meaning of the fable bodied forth in the play as a whole, was robbed of its dramatic validity. It was, indeed, 'a vanity'.

Nevertheless, despite this, we must be grateful to all the artists concerned in this controversial interpretation of the play for re-vealing in a manner not achieved before how deliberately and successfully Shakespeare had incorporated the fully developed Jonsonian masque, complete with anti-masque, into the fabric of *The Tempest*, and for thus alerting those who saw the production to the likely dramatic purpose of both the phantom banquet of Act III and the heavenly vision of Act IV. Instead of being left to consider each of these visual diversions singly and in isolation, we were invited to view them in conjunction, one as the sequel of the other; and simply to have to do this is to have acquired a new critical dimension in which to approach the dramatic possi-bilities of the play, since it forces us to ask whether Shakespeare contented himself with the successful technical achievement of weaving a masque and anti-masque into the text of his play, or whether the purpose of setting himself this task at all was to pro-vide himself with the means to spell out in the fashionable court hieroglyphics of the day the political, philosophical and theologi-cal undertones of this enchanting theatrical romance. The answer, as I believe, is self-evident and is to be found in the stage-directions and the iconography of the masque and anti-masque taken in conjunction as I shall now attempt to show.

The sole controlling agent of both anti-masque and masque in *The Tempest* is, quite properly, Prospero; he provides the former in the harpies' banquet for the discomfiture of the usurper Antonio, the treacherous Alonso and the murderously-intentioned Sebastian: by contrast he offers the masque as entertainment and reward to Ferdinand and Miranda as they emerge freshly tried and tested in the innocence and purity of their love and mutual esteem. Contrary to the conventions of Jonson's masques, some ninety lines of dialogue divorce anti-masque from masque in *The Tempest*; but as it is a stage-play, this is a necessary deviation to permit one set of characters to react to the first vision and then quit the stage in order to make way for those other characters who are to witness the second of Prospero's 'high charms' and who must first be prepared by him to receive it. In other words Shakespeare has to change his audience as well as his setting and his characters.

For the reader this separation appears the more marked because of the obtrusive (and probably fortuitous) break between Acts III and IV which occurs at this point in the Folio text. This serves to distract us today from noticing the far more remarkable fact that Shakespeare should have chosen to borrow this double-device within a year and a half of the invention of anti-masque. Jonson first used it in *The Masque of Queens* (February 2nd, 1609) and took the trouble, in the printed descriptive preface, to define both how he came to include this 'foil, or false masque' at Queen Anne's personal request, and his own intention in interpreting this foil or contrast as 'a spectacle of strangeness, producing multiplicity of gesture, and not unaptly sorting with the current, and whole fall of the device.'[1]

The Tempest was acted at Court on November 1st, 1611, and it is clear from the references in the stage-directions in III.3. to 'strange music' and 'strange shapes', and to the 'gentle actions of salutation' and 'mocks and mows' that Shakespeare was fully conversant with Jonson's views on the nature and purpose of an anti-masque—so well informed (as close comparison of these quotations reveals) as to make one suspect that he had a copy of *The Masque*

[1] See Jonson's *Works*, ed. C. Herford and P. & E. Simpson, vii, 282.

of Queens near to hand when he penned this scene. Moreover, the phantom banquet which, like a mirage, appears only to disappear, mirrors the unnatural and disorderly spiritual state of the 'three men of sin' for whom it is displayed—royal persons whose crimes and hypocrisy make them unfit to govern—and is, indeed, 'not unaptly sorting with the current, and whole fall of the device' when directly contrasted with the proven virtue of Ferdinand and his betrothed for whom the masque proper is reserved:

> All thy vexations
> Were but my trials of thy love, and thou
> Hast strangely stood the test:
> (iv. i. 5–7)

The masque of Goddesses which is their reward, like the anti-masque of harpies, fulfils all the essential requirements of the genre—choreographic compliment ornamented with appropriate songs, dialogue and spectacle directly addressed to the principal witnesses, and congruent in its iconography to them, both as individuals and as political figure-heads.

As I have already observed, the key that unlocks the meaning of a masque is its iconography: so let us next examine this in detail.

Shakespeare employs three solo artists, two as presenters and one as principal, supported by a chorus: Iris and Ceres present Juno who is escorted by water-nymphs and harvesters. The whole stage-picture is pleasing to the eye, mythological, classical, arcadian. Was it ever intended to be more than that? The linking of masque to anti-masque suggests that it was, and the choice of Juno as the central figure presented by Iris strongly reinforces this belief.

Juno, in Peter Hall's production, was unfortunately dressed to resemble Elizabeth I; for in Jacobean iconography Juno was recognized as the Goddess of Union and patroness of marriage, and was thus the last of all the Olympian deities whom any artist of the period would have employed in order to allude to the Virgin Queen. Shakespeare knew better than that. Within the

emblematic imagery of his time his credentials for using Iris as his
Presenter and Juno to preside over the betrothal of Ferdinand and
Miranda are impeccable: for behind both ideas lies Jonson's *Masque
of Hymen* of 1606, the opening stage-direction of which describes,

> an altar; upon which was described in letters of gold,
> Ioni Oimae Mimae
> UNIONI
> SACR.[1]

To this Jonson added a footnote:

> Mystically implying that both it, the place,
> and all the succeeding ceremonies were sacred to
> marriage or Union: over which Juno was president . . .

This message is further spelt out in the stage-direction accompanying Juno's entrance and in the following dialogue.

> Here the upper part of the scene, which was all of
> clouds . . . began to open; and the air clearing,
> in the top thereof was discovered Juno, sitting in a throne
> supported by two beautiful peacocks, her attire rich, and
> like a queen. . . .

Reason, remarking this spectacular apparition, then declares,

> And see where Juno, whose great name
> Is Unio, in the anagram,
> Displays her glittering state and chair.
> As she enlightened all the air.

She is escorted by Iris on her rainbow.

Here then is precedent indeed for the characters of Juno and
Iris in *The Tempest*, not only in their function, but also in the visual
trappings with which they are adorned and presented to public

---

[1] For this and the following quotations see Jonson's *Works, ed. cit.*, vii, 210
et seq.

The Rainbow portrait of Queen Elizabeth I,
Hatfield House, Hertfordshire
see note opposite

view:[1] in Iris, moreover, if not in Juno, Shakespeare had precedent for a direct allusion to Queen Elizabeth I, for it is in this role that she is figured by the anonymous painter of the famous 'Rainbow' portrait at Hatfield House (see plate opposite). The Latin superscription 'Iris: non sine sole' provides the reason for assigning Elizabeth this role.

In Prospero's masque Iris's role is that of Presenter, the prime figure in a tableau of Annunciation: riding 'the watery arch' of the rainbow, itself the time-honoured symbol of peace, harmony and concord, her task is to summon Ceres whose cornucopia was the no less commonly accepted emblem of harvest, prosperity and plenty. These emblems serve in themselves to alert the spectator

[1] The image must have been a striking one for Jonson recalls it (whether in the context of his own masque or in that of *The Tempest*) in his 'Expostulation with Inigo Jones' some ten years later.

> '... I have met with those
> That do cry up the machine, and the shows;
> The majesty of Juno in the clouds,
> And peering forth of Iris in the shrouds,
> ...'

A NOTE ON THE 'RAINBOW' PORTRAIT (*see Plate opposite*)

This portrait of the Queen in the role of Iris was painted during her last years, possibly by Marcus Gheeraetts. The face is taken from Nicholas Hilliard's 'Mask of Youth' miniatures. Every item of the costume is an emblem of the Queen's attributes built around the superscripture *Iris: Non Sine Sole*. The double rainbow—the one in her headdress, the other the prop for her right hand—is the emblem of Peace; but the rainbow is invisible without the light of the sun, itself the emblem of Jupiter and Imperial Majesty.

The Queen's gown is embroidered with eyes, ears, lips and tongues, the emblems of Fame. The bodice is covered with flowers, all of them emblems of either Jupiter or the Virgin Mary—oak, heartsease, honeysuckle, rose, carnation and hyssop.

The elaborately embossed snake and heart on the sleeve represents, in Renaissance iconography, 'Intelligence' and 'Prudence'; but in Christian iconography the serpent was associated with 'Sacred Love' and with 'Truth'. In this instance the latter interpretation is the more likely since Elizabeth's personal motto was *Veritas Filia Temporis*, and this would account for the prominence given to this device in the portrait, thus counterbalancing the rainbow and the superscripture. The moon in the headdress is a normal emblem for Diana, the Virgin Mary and Chastity. The gauntlet on the collar is more problematical, but suggests a reference to the words *Fidei Defensor* in the Queen's title and thus to her championship of the Protestant faith in Europe.

to the particular nature of the Advent thus ceremoniously heralded: for by 1611 few Jacobean Londoners would have failed to recognize this figurative coupling of 'peace' and 'plenty' as the personal insignia of *Beatus Pacificus*, the lion out of Scotland, who had become the English Jupiter as James the sixth and first. This image he had planted in his subjects' minds himself.

I know not by what fortune the diction of *Pacificus* was added to my title at my coming to England, that of lion, expressing true fortitude, having been my diction before. But I am not ashamed of this addition. For King Solomon was a figure of Christ in that he was a King of peace. The greatest gift that our Saviour gave his apostles immediately before His ascension was that he left His Peace with them.[1]

Iris and Ceres therefore, as presented in conjunction in *The Tempest*, figure the peace and prosperity that for the British people is the product of the Union of the Scottish and the English Crowns; and in a masque of ladies this must be figured by Juno, Goddess of Union and thus of marriage in her own right, who now appears in both capacities at once at Prospero's bidding accurately depicted for the audience as 'the Queen o' th' Sky' whose 'peacocks fly amain', just as Jonson's Juno had done in *Hymenaei* with Inigo Jones's assistance and before a similar audience some five years earlier. All is thus prepared when Ceres proclaims

Highest Queen of State
Great Juno comes

for the Court audience to recognize the face behind the symbolic mask of the goddess, as that of Anne, Queen, consort and mother Lest any remain in doubt, Shakespeare provides her with an escort of 'nymphs, called Naiads, of the winding brooks With your . . . sedged crowns and ever-harmless looks', an emblem he took over from Samuel Daniel's masque of the preceding year (June, 1610) *Tethys' Festival* in which Queen Anne had herself

[1] See D. H. Wilson, *King James VI and I*, Cape, 1959 (Reprint: 1962), p. 272.

appeared as Tethys, and the Princess Elizabeth as the River Thames, attended by other rivers.[1] Such was the impact of that vision on contemporary society that Arthur Wilson in his *Life of James I* could write of Anne:

> She was not without some Grandees to attend her for outward *glory*: the Court being a continued *Maskardo*, where she and her Ladies, like so many Sea-Nymphs, or *Nereides*, appeared often in various *dresses* to the *ravishment* of the *beholders*.[2]

The pressure therefore on audiences of the time to recognize within the figure of Juno that of Queen Anne was overwhelming. And if one of the children whom she has come to bless on stage is Prospero's daughter, that same child, in the figurative manner of masque, is also her own—the next Elizabeth, Princess Royal, and godchild of Elizabeth I, and the most eligible bride in Europe described by Sir Henry Wotton as 'th' eclipse and glory of her kind' and by Shakespeare as Miranda. Just as appropriate if only slightly more oblique are the allusions to King James in the pun on 'prosperity' in Prospero, and in the equation of Prospero's 'high charms' with those of the author of *Daemonologie*.

If then, at this extraordinary moment of the play's climax, the two Elizabeths (dead monarch and marriageable Princess), Queen Anne and James I are all to be seen on the stage together as

---

[1] Samuel Daniel, *Complete Works in Verse and Prose*, ed. A. B. Grosart, 5 vols. (London 1885–96; reprinted New York, 1963). King James figures in that Masque (which was specially commissioned for the investiture of Henry as Prince of Wales) as Ocean's King. Tethys explains that she and her attendant rivers have recently visited Milford Haven,

> The happy Port of Union, which gave way
> To that great Hero HENRY (i.e. Henry VII), and his fleete,
> To make that blest conjunction that begat
> A greater, and more glorious far than that.
> III. 314

It is for this reason of course that Milford Haven is referred to by Shakespeare in *Cymbeline* as 'blessed'.

[2] See Arthur Wilson, *The History of Great Britain being the Life and Reign of King James the First*, London, 1653, pp. 53–4.

flickering images in the mirror of the masque's received conventions, who then is the other mortal whom Juno has come to bless at Prospero's request?

In November, 1611, this must have been the most tantalizing component of the whole device. By then three candidates for this role could be eliminated; the King of Sweden, the Duke of Brunswick and the Prince of Nassau. All had been suitors but had been dismissed.[1]

Two other candidates, however, were both pressing their claims, the Protestant Elector Palatine supported by James, and the Catholic Prince of Piedmont, heir to the Duke of Savoy, backed by Queen Anne: dark rumours were also circulating in Court circles of a third suitor eclipsing both in power and prestige—the recently widowed Philip III, King of Spain.[2]

James had made peace with Spain in 1604 With this achieved and with Parliament, after five years of wrangling, having finally agreed to the Union of the Scottish with the English Crown in 1608, James was free to pursue his self-appointed role of peacemaker by endeavouring to reunite a divided Christendom through dynastic marriages which, as the father of a daughter and two sons, he was well placed to attempt as every embassy in Europe knew well.

Come they (i.e. other nations) not hither (i.e. to London) as to the fountain from whence peace springs? Here sits Solomon and hither come the tribes for judgement. O happy moderator,

---

[1] See E. C. Williams, *Anne of Denmark*, Longman, 1970, p. 153.

[2] See *Calender of State Papers (Domestic) James I*, 2073 (221) 1611–1618, p. 89. No. 35. November 18th, Newmarket, Humph. May to Salisbury.

> Has delivered the despatch from France and complemented the King (i.e. James) that two great Princes offer him their alliance for the Princess. His Majesty wishes the negotiation with the Elector Palatine to proceed by the Duke of Bouillon, and will reply to the Ambassador of Savoy after he has spoken with that of Spain. His Ambassador in Spain is to condole with that King (i.e. on his Queen's death).

The oil painting, attributed to M. Gheeraedts, of the signing of the Peace Treaty in London is reproduced by E. C. Williams, *op. cit.*

blessed Father, not Father of thy country alone, but Father of all thy neighbour countries about thee.[1]

If 'Father' strikes us as an extravagant image, we must recall that 'Father-in-Law' could easily become the literal truth.

All three candidates who were being canvassed for the role of prospective fiancé in the winter of 1611 are interesting: Frederick, Count Palatine because he was destined to become the bridegroom eighteen months later and because Queen Anne was strongly opposed to disposing of her only daughter to a mere Count: Philip of Spain because the glamour of the prospective dowry was matched by deep seated fear and mistrust of the Pope's most fanatical champion in the minds of Lord Treasurer Salisbury and most of his closest associates: the Prince of Piedmont, not only because of the exotic gifts including a leopard and two white bears presented by his father, the Duke of Savoy, to James I and placed in the care of Philip Henslowe and Edward Alleyn in 1610, but because of an especially fascinating item of gossip associated with his prospects. This is documented in the *Calendar of State Papers* (*Domestic*) among a group of opinions on 'suitable alliances for the Prince of Wales and the Princess Elizabeth'. It reads as follows:

> The Prince of Piedmont an unequal match for the Princess, unless the King of Spain will give him the Duchy of Milan on his marriage which is not likely as that King is said to want her for himself.

What then are we to conclude about the figure of Ferdinand in *The Tempest* and the living face behind the stage-mask? I am myself loathe to believe that Shakespeare had only one of the three principal candidates in mind and no other: rather is it likely that he chose to be ambiguous and to give his audience the fun of trying to identify their favourite candidate and to leave each faction to argue its own case with their rivals after this insubstantial pageant had faded from view. When the play was revived at Court on

[1] See D. H. Wilson, *op. cit.* p. 272, citing Robert Aylett, *Peace and Her Foure Gardens*, 1622.

February 14th, 1613, for the festivities marking the wedding of the Princess, then of course Ferdinand could only have been equated with the Elector Palatine; but that was at another time and is another story.[1] What must be taken into account, in November 1611, is the clearly documented possibility that Shakespeare elected to batten upon the masque and the newly minted anti-masque, and to couple them together as a single dramatic device in *The Tempest*, in order to give himself the chance to comment in the manner fashionable at the time on the most topical and controversial issue of contemporary foreign and domestic policy. What then emerges is a vivid allegorical charade in the conventional style of the old dumb-shows, but brilliantly updated and dressed out in the novel and spectacular court-hieroglyphics of the Jonsonian masque.

Although strictly confined to the limits of the two choreo-graphic tableaux, the allusions to the royal patron, his family, his achievements and intentions spill obliquely into other aspects of the play. If, in Prospero's faith and magic powers deployed in substituting forgiveness, peace and reconcilement for revenge and the consequent tragedies for mankind of recurrent deaths and everlasting war, a correspondence may be seen to the diplomatic skills and aspirations of the Kingly peacemaker and author of the *Daemonologie*, so can a reference be glimpsed in Caliban's plot on his life to the Gunpowder treason; Prospero's isle, moreover, may itself be regarded as the Great Britain of James's making on whose shores the naval forces of its Catholic enemies were wrecked by storms, but within whose bounds, by the process of dynastic alliances in the marriage of children, reconcilement of former differences is to be achieved and a prosperous future ensured for all.

---

[1] Choice of the name Ferdinand strikes me as deliberate and intended to re-call Ferdinand of Aragon who, in marrying Isabella of Castille in 1469, united Spain. A similar Union between Spain and England was effected by the wedding of their daughter, Catherine of Aragon, first to Prince Arthur and then to Henry VIII. This was not a subject that could be discussed either at Court, or in a play while Queen Elizabeth I was alive; but by 1611 it could, more especially in the context of *The Tempest*, and accords with Shakespeare's own efforts in his next play, *Henry VIII*, to re-establish Catherine as a woman more sinned against than sinning.

In 1611 these achievements—reconcilement of Protestants with Catholics and of Britain with the continent of Europe—were still dreams awaiting fulfilment: but as prospects that could follow upon the more modest diplomatic successes of the peace with Spain and the Union of the Scottish with the English Crown they pointed the way to a more optimistic future than had been thinkable for generations: as such they merited acknowledgement, if not in the extravagant terms of the apotheosis later accorded to James in the ceiling of the Banquet Hall in Whitehall (paid for by Charles I and painted by Rubens) then at least in terms of the state spectacle that had by then become the normal function of a Court Masque.[1]

Thus the closing scene and Epilogue serve simultaneously both to conduct the audience gently away from the enchanted, make-believe world of masque and play towards the harsher environment of real life, and as an apotheosis of the sovereign before the eyes of the assembled Court. That James has brought peace to Britain no one can deny: that he may yet bring it to the rest of Europe through the flower of modern chivalry, Henry, Prince of Wales, and a paragon of feminine beauty, grace and wit, the Princess Elizabeth, is still an undeniable possibility if men will only follow James's example in abjuring revenge and placing their faith in the 'brave new world' of the younger generation: wage peace, not war. Yet spectators are also asked to recall that the sovereign, despite his diplomatic successes, his literary achievements and Divine Right, is mortal man, a compound of pure and impure elements, body and soul, and thus as much a victim of circumstance in the harsh world of reality.

Prospero is thus slowly stripped of all the artificial supernatural aids on which, within the magic world of play, his successes had depended: the reappearance of the Boatswain and his crew serve to recall the grim realism of the storm in the opening scene and thus the actual worlds of Naples, Milan and political responsibilities in

---

[1] One panel out of the total of nine is reproduced in *Elizabethan Theatre III* ed. David Galloway: see n. 2, p. 2. The fullest discussion of Rubens's commission, together with elaborate illustration, is provided by Per Palme, *The Triumphe of Peace: A Study of the Whitehall Banqueting House,* Stockholm, 1956.

which Ferdinand and Miranda will live their married lives. Masque and anti-masque have served, like mists parting to reveal a mountain only to roll back again and shroud it from sight, to provide a mystical transfiguration that the departing audience must ponder for themselves. *The Tempest* thus emerges at all levels—from simple, theatrical romance, via allusive political commentary to metaphysical discourse—as a single unified work of art firmly held together by the successful incorporation of a masque and anti-masque within the dramatic structure of a stage-play. It does so in the Baroque manner, richly encrusted with fanciful ornament in narrative, spectacle and tragi-comic form; a manner intended simultaneously to delight and instruct in equal measure and as nearly in keeping with Sir Philip Sidney's requirements of dramatic poetry as may be imagined.

II

Robert South and the Augustans

IRÈNE SIMON

In a recent study Paul Fussell has shown that the Augustan humanists' response to the eighteenth century was 'anachronistic and reactionary':[1] while the newer trends of thought associated with deism and benevolism were readily espoused by the 'optimists', the Augustans held fast to a conception of man and of his moral responsibility based on orthodox Christian doctrine. The opposition appears most clearly if we compare Swift's wry praise of 'The Serene Peaceful State, of being a Fool among Knaves',[2] which reveals his profound discomfort, with Addison's praise of cheerfulness,[3] which shows how easy it was for him to come to terms with the world around him, even though he hoped to improve it by gently laughing at its follies. Addison's high regard for Tillotson, as well as the main burden of his own lay sermons, points to the influence of the Latitudinarians, from whose thought the liberal theology of the eighteenth century took its rise. On the other hand, as a High-Churchman, Swift was closer to the more conservative Restoration divines who staunchly opposed all accommodations with the Dissenters; indeed, in his sermons *On Brotherly Love* (1717) and on *The Martyrdom of King Charles I* (1726) he uses the same arguments and speaks with the same violence as the Restoration preacher who was known in his time as the scourge of the fanatics, Robert South. No doubt both Swift and South were driven by partisan zeal, but in attacking enthusiasm they were also fighting against the disruptive forces of modernism. If *A Tale of a Tub* is the most brilliant exposure

[1] Paul Fussell: *The Rhetorical World of Augustan Humanism. Ethics and Imagery from Swift to Burke.* Oxford, 1965, p. 20.
[2] *A Tale of a Tub*, ed. Herbert-Davis, *The Prose Writings of Jonathan Swift*, Oxford, 1957, I. 110.
[3] *Spectator*, no. 370.

of self-assertion in literature and in religion, the standards against which such errors are measured are most readily grasped in the sermons of South. These, indeed, provide a consistent body of doctrine and develop the main themes of the Augustan ethos.

As Louis I. Bredvold[1] has shown, the gloom of the Tory satirists was not the expression of some vague melancholia, but of their sense that man was reverting to the subhuman and that the cultural heritage was threatened by the inroads of the puny insects which, in Pope's *Dunciad*, swarm round the throne of Dulness. South had witnessed the chaos of the Interregnum, and his outspoken defence of humanist values was clearly prompted by the fear that civilized order might once more collapse. This sense of a threat to man as a rational creature pervades the works of the Augustan humanists from Swift to Burke and, as Fussell has demonstrated, is the source of their imagery of warfare. South's evocation of the King tried by the rabble and torn like an Actaeon by a pack of bloodhounds[2] arouses the same horror and indignation as Burke felt for the mob's treatment of the Archbishop of Rouen. His insistence that learning is a prerequisite to preaching (IV, sermon 1) may be paralleled with Pope's advice to the poet, and his condemnation of extempore prayers (II, sermons 3 and 4) on the ground that premeditation and control intensify the feelings may be read as a recommendation to join art to nature, while his repeated stress on the need to exercise discipline on both reason and the will, and to guard against loose thinking as well as against the deceitfulness of the heart, reminds us of Johnson's many admonitions to Boswell. Finally, his belief in a hierarchic principle, in man as in society, is as inseparable from his belief in the dignity of man as are Swift's assumptions in *Meditation upon a Broomstick*, or Pope's in *An Essay on Man*, or Burke's in his animadversions upon *The*

    [1] Louis I. Bredvold: 'The Gloom of the Tory Satirists', in *Pope and his Contemporaries, Essays presented to George Sherburn*, ed. James L. Clifford and Louis A. Landa, Oxford, 1949.
    [2] Robert South: *Sermons Preached upon Several Occasions*. 6th ed., London, 1727, 6 vols; I, sermon 2. Further references, in parentheses in the text, are to this edition, identified by volume number and page or by volume number and sermon number.

Rights of Man; it is this principle that the Aeolists flout when boasting of the inspirations they owe 'to certain subterraneous *Effluviums* of *Wind*'[1] and that Dulness denies when she encourages her sons to study flies. For South man is indeed the glory of the world since he was created in the image of God and has within him the Candle of the Lord; but if he is to remain worthy of this trust he must exercise discipline and, as a free and responsible agent, conform his thoughts and actions to right reason, for only thus can he be truly human.

The foundation of South's ethos is his belief—which needed to be asserted the more emphatically in order to counter the growth of philosophical scepticism and of moral relativism in mid-seventeenth century—in the objective nature of truth and good-ness. Truth consists in the conformity of our ideas to the things of which they are the images (II, 334); good and evil inhere in the things themselves, they are founded neither on opinion nor, as Hobbes claimed, 'in the Laws and Constitutions of the Sovereign Civil Power' (II, 324). Moral goodness, like truth, is thus absolute and uniform. Evil must be combated even though the civil power may tolerate it (e.g. Nonconformity) or fail to devise laws against it (e.g. lying). As a preacher South had to exhort men to reform their lives and to warn them against sin, but he was more violent than most in condemning all swerving from the right path. If in his denunciation of abuses he was often driven to bitter sarcasm and invective, he might well have given the same justification as Pope: 'Ask you what Provocation I have had? The strong Antipathy of Good to Bad'.[2]

Since the Fall, man no longer enjoys that 'Rectitude of all the Faculties of the Soul, by which they stand apt and disposed to their respective Offices and Operations' (I, 50); but since God has implanted in him the common notions, which are the basis of all reasoning, he can, through the right use of reason, arrive at the truths of natural religion and also grasp that it is in the nature

---

[1] *A Tale of a Tub*, ed. cit., I. 99.
[2] Epilogue to the Satires, Dialogue II, l. 197, in *Imitations of Horace*, ed. John Butt, The Twickenham Edition of the Poems of Alexander Pope, IV, London, 1953.

of a perfectly wise and good God to have revealed his word to man; hence he can accept Scripture as the word of God. For South as for his fellow-Anglicans faith is a rational assent to truths revealed, upon recognition of the veracity and goodness of God. All unbelief is ultimately to be traced to the 'pravity' of the will, which can hinder the exercise of the understanding. This, in South's view, is the cause of atheism and scepticism. If the Jews rejected Christ's doctrine, he explains, it was not because the arguments were insufficient, nor because the natural light of man's understanding is defective, but because the doctrine of self-denial 'came upon the World, like Light darting full upon the Face of a Man asleep, who had a Mind to sleep on, and not to be disturbed' (I, 222). The will cannot choose evil, for 'a suitable, or proper *Good* being proposed to it, it has a Power to refuse, or not to chuse it; yet it has no Power to chuse *Evil*, considered absolutely as *Evil*' (II, 317). It may, however, be led into such a choice because the understanding represents to it 'things really *Evil*, under the Notion and Character of *Good*' (II, 317). The question is then: why or how does the understanding sometimes mislead the will? First, because it is apt to be deceived by words when these are distorted from their true function, that is, are not true signs of things. This is what South calls 'the imposture of words', and he preached several sermons on this theme to warn against Puritan catchphrases such as 'liberty of conscience' (cp. Swift on the meaning of 'moderation' in his sermon *On Brotherly Love*, where he shows the folly of those 'who are made the Tools and Instruments of [their] Betters, to work their Designs').[1] The second source of deceit lies in the will itself, for though it is free 'to apply the understanding Faculty to, or to take it off from the Consideration' of any object (I, 232), it may through slothfulness allow the passions to prevail and sin to darken the understanding; when man's judgment is swayed by his passions, the light within is turned to darkness (III, 54ff). Although reason naturally conforms to truth and the will naturally chooses good, both are thus apt to be distorted from their right ends; if South now stresses the proneness of the will to evil, now the errors of the understanding,

[1] *Sermons*, ed. Louis Landa, *The Prose Writings*, ed. cit., XI, 173.

the contradiction is only apparent, for his main object is to emphasize the need for vigilance and discipline in order to rectify the judgment *and* to purge the heart. This is a commonplace of Christian teaching, but what characterizes South is his call to constant alertness, his warning against all forms of loose thinking, and his insistence that man free his will from its prepossessions, for then it 'will engage the *Mind* in a severe Search' after truth (I, 238). The energy and perseverance required in this inquiry are expressed through an image which looks forward to the many metaphors of moral warfare used by the Augustans:

> Truth is a great Strong-hold, barred and fortified by God and Nature; and Diligence is properly the Understanding's laying Siege to it: So that, as in a Kind of Warfare, it must be perpetually upon the Watch; observing all the Avenues and Passes to it, and accordingly makes its Approaches. Sometimes it thinks it gains a Point; and presently again, it finds its self baffled and beaten off: Yet still it renews the Onset; attacks the Difficulty afresh; plants this Reasoning, and that Argument, this Consequence, and that Distinction, like so many intellectual Batteries, till at length it forces a Way and Passage into the obstinate enclosed Truth, that so long withstood, and defied all its Assaults.
>
> (I, 239–40)

South was thus led to emphasize both the will's proneness to evil and its redemptive power. As a preacher he was bound to remind his congregation that man is a free agent responsible for his moral choices and therefore that he must exercise control over his passions—that is, rectify his will. Like his fellow-Anglicans he rejected the doctrine of predestination because it is a slur upon the equity and Goodness of God (I, 59); more specifically he denounced those aspects of it which led to antinomianism and thereby resulted in a reversion to animality. Like all Christian teachers he also stressed the danger of committing the conduct of life to the heart, because it is weak and deceitful. Not that all passions are deviations from right reason, as the Stoics believed (II, 67); indeed they are necessary to move to action, but they are

'apt to pass into excess' (III, 68) and therefore need the strong discipline of reason. Although this is again a commonplace, the
sermon South preached on the text of *Prov.* xxviii. 26, *He who
trusteth in his own Heart is a Fool*, may be compared with Swift's
On the Testimony of Conscience, which glances at Shaftesbury's
doctrine of benevolence, and South may have chosen to include it,
together with seven *Discourses on Temptation*, in the last volume
he prepared for the press (published 1717) because of its topical
interest. Besides, the impact of this search is comparable to that of
several others in which he deals with conscience as sole guide to
the good life, and the main drift is the same all through: man is
not to trust his own powers but to check his private judgment
against the authority of universal reason or of Scripture. And this
again is the basis of his attack against 'enthusiasm'.

Like his fellow-Anglicans South believed that the truths of religion are received upon the assent of reason, either directly or
mediately (through recognition that Scripture is the word of God);
like them too he opposed the doctrine of implicit faith: man
needs no external infallible guide—the Pope—to tell him what to
believe, since his own reason when properly exercised cannot but
show him the truths necessary for salvation. Not all men are able
to read Scripture correctly; the ministers are to be their guides in
interpreting the credenda of religion and they too need learning in
order not to mistake the true sense of the word of God. However,
all men are encouraged to exercise their judgment, for they cannot
remit to others the responsibility of believing the right doctrine.
It is therefore fit for the preacher to address himself to the understanding of his congregation and to lay out the truths of Christianity. Reliance on the private judgment is, however, directly
opposed to the claims of the 'fanatics' to follow no other guide
than their private conscience. South repeatedly refers to the
extravagant notions which illiterate people read into Scripture,
and he also ridicules the mysterious doctrines that some Puritans
extract from it (e.g. 'recumbency' or 'rolling in Christ'). He heaps
irony and abuse on all claims to inspiration, and many of his
sermons recall Swift's analysis of Aeolism and his Digression upon
madness. Forgetting that man is 'a being darkly wise, and rudely

great',[1] the enthusiasts pretend to direct intuition of God (v, 305); but these 'seraphic pretenders' (v, 292) reveal their true nature when, in preaching by the spirit, they either flutter in the air 'by a kind of vain empty Lightness, or lie grovelling upon the Ground, by a dead and contemptible Flatness' (IV, 49–50). Elsewhere, South compares the Spirit dwelling in them to 'an admirable kind of invisible *Clock-work* moving them, just as a Spring does a Watch' (II, 206; cp. Swift's *Mechanical Operations of the Spirit*); or again to men with 'the gift of *Talking in their Sleep*, or Dreaming while *they are awake*' (IV, 413).[2] Such pretences cannot be a sure ground on which to build the good life; rather they lead men into whirlpools where they turn and turn until they are seized with giddiness (IV, 414). No wonder the fanatics' prayers should be 'so full of Ramble, and Inconsequence', and spoken with '*Eyes* for the most part shut, and [. . .] *Arms* out in a yawning Posture' (II, 159–60), or accompanied with 'Distortion of Face, sanctified Grimace, solemn Wink, or foaming at the Mouth' (II, 95–6). No wonder the poor tools of such ministers of the Gospel should become mere beasts, hounds whose throats, nose and fangs are used to run the quarry down (IV, 501). The various comparisons South uses emphasize the reversal to the subhuman, as indeed do the actions which such pretences are meant to justify. The point is that, in obeying such motions, men renounce man's prerogative, reason, cease to be free agents, and become the mere toys of their passions. Something of Swift's æolism is implied in one of South's compressed images: '*new Lights, sudden Impulses of the Spirit, extraordinary Calls*, will be but weak Arguments to prove any Thing but the Madness of those that use them, and that the Church must needs wither, being *blasted* with such *Inspirations*' (I, 151).

Although this is standard practice in the rhetoric of abuse, South grounds his censure of enthusiasm in the distinction between the private exercise of right reason and private illuminations: for

---

[1] Pope: *An Essay on Man*, II, 4.

[2] Paul Fussell (*op. cit.* p. 106) quotes a paragraph from *Decline and Fall* (ch. XV) on the alleged visionary powers of the early Christians, in which Gibbon uses a similar image.

since reason is shared by all men (though in different degrees) and since truth is a conformity to the nature of things, the 'truths' revealed to the individual through the Spirit dwelling in him should be amenable to reason. Yet the enthusiasts can give no evidence of these truths to others: they plead *'that the Spirit leads them by an inward Voice speaking to them, and known only to themselves'* (v, 289); they cannot stand the test of reason, so that what they take for the voice of the Spirit can be no more than 'the dictates of [their] own Mind or Fancy' (v, 298), which authorize them to do what they please. Indeed the enthusiasts themselves 'lay the Foundation of this Pretence in the Ruins of Reason' (v, 299). As the light of nature, right reason is the intellectual power or faculty of the soul that directs man to truth; as the law of nature, it obliges man to do good. By setting their own private motions above reason, the enthusiasts nullify all law. That this inevitably leads to anarchy South can show only too easily by referring to the late confusions in Church and State. And he can also show that one of the logical conclusions of trust in private motions is antinomianism, which makes good and evil relative to the quality of the agent, i.e. depending upon whether he is regenerate or not (II, 205). However much South may be driven by his partisan zeal, it is clear that his attitude is quite consistent, given his belief in the objective nature of truth and goodness, and in the conformity of right reason to truth.

Reason is indeed 'a Ray of Divinity darted into the Soul' (II, 417), but once man has recognized that Scripture is the word of God, he is committed to accepting the truths revealed in Scripture even if his reason cannot properly comprehend them. The mysteries of religion are beyond, though not against, reason; to deny them is to doubt the veracity of God; to pry into them is sheer madness: 'Christ demands the Homage of your Understanding: He will have your *Reason* bend to him, you must put your Heads under his Feet' (I, 93). Not only in the realm of religion but in the natural world what is not comprehensible to human reason is not therefore impossible: who, South asks, can 'give a full Account of how *Sensation is performed*' (III, 248). It is therefore extravagant presumption to pretend to clear up all mysteries; only an unruly and over-curious reason will try to solve these difficulties, and 'he that too much strives to understand [the mystery of the Trinity], may lose *his Wits*' (IV, 306). The danger of speculations such as those in which the Schoolmen indulged is that they undermine belief in the mysteries; indeed 'unjustifiable notions' concerning the divine essence and person, he says, 'caused in *Socinus* such an high loathing of, and Aversion to that whole Scheme of Christian Theology, which then obtained in the World, that breaking through all, he utterly deny'd the divine Nature *of the Son*, and *of the Holy Ghost*' (V, 122). South's warning echoes Raphael's to Adam to be 'lowly wise' and looks forward to Pope's words: 'to reason right, is to submit'.[1] South preached several sermons on the mysteries of religion, and at the time of the Trinitarian controversy took issue with those divines whose speculations on the nature of the Trinity only brought grist to the mill of their opponents. In an early sermon (1659) he had already stated that all disputes about the Trinity 'arise only from Curiosity and Singularity' and he viewed these as 'Faults of a diseased Will' (I, 91). 'Singularity' is censured as implying dissent from universal wisdom, i.e. as a straying from the path of nature or right reason. Such an assertion of self is dangerous since it sets the individual judgment above the universal standards of truth and goodness. Man cannot hope to form an adequate representation of the nature and attributes of God, for 'how can such vast and mighty Things be crowded into a little, finite Understanding!' ... how shall the *King of Glory, whom the Heavens themselves cannot contain, enter in by these Doors?* by a weak Imagination, a slender Notion, and a contracted Intellect?' (III, 215). The credenda of the Christian religion are therefore proposed 'not to our *Knowledge*, but to our *Belief*' (III, 225); to that extent reason must bend to faith, for '*know and understand* [the mysterious Points of our Faith] thoroughly we cannot; but since God has *revealed* and *affirmed* them *to be true*, we may with the highest Reason, upon his bare Word, believe and assent to them as such' (III, 225). Thus, while grounding religion in reason, South also emphasizes the limitations of reason.

[1] *An Essay on Man*, I, 164.

Man is indeed the glory of the world, but he is also a pitiful thing that cannot find means to be delivered from his deepest distress unless he trust in God's wisdom and power: 'by this Means a Man may see his pitiful Narrow Reason *nonpluss'd* and *outdone*, before he sees his Wants answered; and the *proud Nothing* own himself baffled, while in spite of his *Despair* he finds himself *delivered*.' (VI, 263). In the conduct of life reason is to be relied upon and obeyed when it tells us what not to do for '*It is the Candle of the Lord* (as Solomon calls it) and God never lights us up a *Candle* either *to put out*, or *to sleep by*'; it is wrong indeed to imagine 'that either Law or Gospel will absolve, what natural Conscience *condemns*' (II, 417). Yet because the light of reason is only a candle, conscience must be guided by the revealed word of God, particularly with regard to man's positive duties. The danger is, indeed, that mere opinions, or persuasions should be mistaken for dictates of conscience (II, 445). As a consequence, though conscience is the vicegerent of God in man, its promptings must be checked with the word of the authority behind it. Thus, whether viewed as a principle of knowledge or as a guide to action, human reason needs to refer to a higher standard of truth and goodness.

Given South's stress on the limitations of human powers, it is no wonder that he should have viewed with distrust '*Ecstatick* Notions of Religion' (IV, 195) which nullified the doctrine of eternal rewards and punishments. It is true, he says, that virtue is its own reward in this sense that its worth is such as to deserve men's choice of it; but to pretend that men 'in their natural estate' need no incentives to choose virtue and lead the good life is wholly to mistake their nature. Such a 'romantic' doctrine may be applicable 'to the Angels, to the *Cherubims* and *Seraphims*' (IV, 180), but to apply it to men is simply absurd, for 'Duty carries with it a *grim*, and a *severe Aspect*; and the very Nature of it involves *Difficulty*. And *Difficulty*, certainly, is no very apt thing to ingratiate or endear itself to Mens Practices and Affections' (IV, 185). To take away the incitements to duty is to 'dash the performance' of it. It is no use arguing that Christians are not slaves but sons, for though the Gospel has superseded the law of works it has not changed human nature. These '*Seraphick Pretenders to Religion*, who have presumed to refine upon it by such airy, impracticable Notions, and have made such a mighty Noise with their *Gospel-Spirits, and Gospel-Dispensations, their high Attainments, and wonderful Illuminations*' have made it so difficult for man to be good 'that there is no Hope of being a *Christian*, without being something more than a *Man*' (IV, 212). Even these 'High-Flyers' cannot claim to be '*Nothing but a pure ascending Flame*' (IV, 213) and those who do are as likely as not to be urging such claims only to justify their indulgence in their natural propensities; ultimately then, such romantic notions only result in the abasement of man. The sermon on *The Recompense of the Reward*, preached in 1698, in which South refutes such notions, is clearly directed against extreme interpretations of the doctrine of Christian liberty, by the Quakers for instance; but like Swift's *On the Testimony of Conscience* it may be read as a refutation of benevolism and of the theory of man's natural moral sense. The comparison is all the more interesting as it brings out the similarity between the private illuminations of the 'fanatics' and the benevolists' reliance on man's good nature, which both conservative Churchmen staunchly opposed. Although he ridiculed religious enthusiasm, Shaftesbury was to extol another kind of enthusiasm which, like the other, denies the need for checks and controls from divine laws. In defining the role of conscience as well as in upholding the doctrine of eternal rewards and punishments South was defending a position which the Augustan humanists were to find more and more endangered by the 'optimists'. It is characteristic that once again he should have emphasized that the performance of duty is difficult and that to lead the good life is a hard task, because man needs to discipline his natural inclinations. He was in no way prepared either to idealize the condition of man or to foster any easy optimism about man's achievements; but he viewed man as able, with the help of religion, to maintain his dignity as a rational creature.

The morality he preached implies a hierarchy among the objects offered to man's desires, just as his conception of man implies a hierarchy among created beings: man is neither angel nor beast, but according to his moral choices he can ascend or fall in the scale of beings. This sense of degree has its counterpart in his contempt for the rabble and in his fear that the fanatic crew might once more subvert the social order. He never tires of evoking the late confusions in Church and State, and one cannot but sense his scorn for the lower orders as well as his awe before the majesty that hedges a King. Yet his denunciation of the godly or enthusiastic preachers is grounded in the fact that they have had no preparation for the ministry: 'Preaching by the Spirit' is open to anyone who feels himself moved to speak, like an instrument upon which the wind blows. It is a case of the blind leading the blind, i.e. a usurpation of power, in so far as exercise of power implies both gifts and training for the particular work to be done. South is no doubt too ready to regard all the fanatics as 'mechanic rabble', but in his soberer moments he can argue cogently for the need of training in whatever sphere man is called upon to exercise his talents, particularly in the ministry; 'had Preaching been made, and reckoned a Matter of solid and true Learning, of Theological Knowledge, and long, and severe Study (as the Nature of it required it to be), assuredly, no *preaching Cobler* amongst them all, would ever have ventured *so far beyond his Last*, as to undertake it' (IV, 55). He does recognize the variety of gifts, even among the men called to the Church, and he views this as an element of beauty; but he also recognizes that the greater part of mankind are unable 'to judge exactly of Things' (II, 346), partly because they lack 'judging or discerning Abilities' and partly because they lack 'the Leisure and Opportunity to apply their Minds' to considerations that require such a strict study (II, 346); they are therefore unfit to guide themselves, and must needs be led by others. The conclusion he draws from this, however, is that the responsibility of the leaders is all the greater since they may be followed blindly. Those who betray this trust by presenting to the people false notions under favourable words are doing the work of the devil, the father of lies, through whom evil entered into the world, for 'God commanded, and *told Man what was Good*, but the Devil Sir-named it *Evil*' (II, 318). The argument is no less cogent for being offered to counter the Dissenters' plea for liberty of conscience (though an unsympathetic reader might retort that what South is doing is Sir-naming good evil, and therefore also the work of the devil), for what it emphasizes is the danger of misleading others who are not in a position to check the truth of doctrines presented to them, whether in religion or in politics, and therefore the responsibility of those in power towards the people they govern. In this also South foreshadows the Augustans who criticized people in high places for their breach of duty. This is reflected in his own practice as a preacher; like Swift he despised the art of wetting the handkerchief and, rather than try to move the passions, he always addressed himself to the understanding of his congregation, setting forth the truths of religion in as cogent and lucid a way as he could so as to rectify their judgment and will. Moreover he reminded those who have been lifted up 'to a Station of Power' that no man holds the gifts of Heaven as a proprietor, but as a steward, that they are trustees of Providence and that it is therefore their duty to be helpful to society (IV, 74). If South's conception of society reflects his aristocratic temper, it is also one according to which mutual rights and duties, if properly understood, must conduce to harmony. No doubt he was out of step with economic and social changes that were in the long run to alter conceptions of government; but so was the Augustans' resistance to mercantilist society and, ultimately, to theories of the rights of man.

The conception of man and of his role in society that emerges from South's sermons is thus one with which the Augustans were in complete agreement. Man occupies a middle station; he is poised between two infinities, endowed with reason but also prone to evil, capable of ascent if he conform his will to right reason but liable to become a beast if he surrender control to his appetites. In such a perilous position he needs to exercise discipline if he is to remain fully human, and this is an arduous task that requires constant vigilance. These are commonplaces of Christian ethics, but for South as for the Augustans they were the more valuable because they were confirmed by the humanistic tradition. And they needed to be restated vigorously because they were being assailed by newer theories that made man the arbiter of truth, and gratification of self the end of all actions. In no respect is South's temper closer to the Augustans' than in his rejection of the untutored genius, whether as claiming direct inspiration through the 'motions of the Spirit' or as putting its trust in the self-sufficiency of human reason. To the free expression of self he opposed the need for premeditation and control: neither the individual conscience nor the heart is its own lawgiver, any more than genius can rely on its sole light. While the Augustans attempted to define objective standards of taste, he urged man to measure the light of his own reason by the standards of right reason. He valued order and discipline in the ceremonies of the Church as he did in the conduct of life. 'Nothing rude, slight and careless; or, indeed, less than the very best that a Man can offer, can be acceptable or pleasing to God in Prayer' (II, 105), and the very best cannot be achieved by extempore praying any more than by unpremeditated writing. Swift laughed at the spider for being proud of spinning its cobwebs solely out of its own substance; South would have shuddered at such self-sufficiency, as he would at Young's advice to the prospective poet to *reverence* himself.

III

The Actaeon Myth in Shelley's Poetry

JEAN PERRIN

EARLY in his life Shelley was fascinated by the figure of the Wandering Jew. He was probably influenced by the taste of the time and by his readings: *The Rime of the Ancient Mariner*, Wordsworth's *Song for the Wandering Jew*, Southey's *Thalaba* in which Ahasuerus is the mythical background of Aswad, the stranger who meets the hero and tells him the long suffering of 'life in death'.

In 1809, the young Shelley and his cousin Medwin jointly wrote a story entitled *The Wandering Jew*, later turned into verse and inserted into *Queen Mab*. 'Ahasuerus is presented as a Jewish Promethean character who defies the Lord and suffers perpetually but remains unrepentant.'[1] In the first important work of our poet, as in the epic poem which Goethe planned to write, Ahasuerus is 'the man of reason' pitted against God or Fate, a typical Shelleyan hero preferring 'Hell's freedom to the servitude of Heaven'.

Now one of the most fascinating things for the student of poetry is to study the maturing of an image before, or even in the course of, a given poem, or sometimes, as we shall try to show in this essay, the development of a mythical theme into another.

In *Queen Mab*, Ahasuerus appears only in the seventh canto. Yet his arrival is announced at the beginning of the sixth canto, although imperceptibly at a first reading, for he will materialize out of a landscape described as follows:

> It is a wild and miserable world
> Thorny and full of care
>
> (ll. 12–13)

[1] J. Gaer, *The Legend of the Wandering Jew*, p. 119 (A Mentor Book, 1961).

I shall deal later with some details which herald the *Ode to the West Wind*. Then Ianthe's Spirit asks:

> O Fairy! In the lapse of years,
> Is there no hope in store?
> Will yon vast suns roll on
> Interminably, still illumining wretched souls,
> And see no hope for them?
>
> (ll. 15–20)

already evoking the theme of hopeless, infinite wandering, and depicts a hostile setting which is completed and accentuated a hundred lines further on, in the style of *Alastor*: a wild, roaring storm sweeps over human life and across the universe, the storm of change guided by an irresistible, determined force; and in the work of the raging elements, in what seems to be sheer anarchy to the shipwrecked sailor, there is not a single detail that does not serve a definite purpose (vi, ll. 156–173). It is the usual, legendary setting of the Wandering Jew, magnified to the dimensions of life.[1] Ahasuerus, who is soon conjured up by the Fairy, becomes the symbol of a whole aspect of mankind:

> A strange and woe-worn wight
> . . . .
> The wisdom of old age was mingled there
> With youth's primeval dauntlessness.
>
> (vii, ll. 68, 78–79)

For the first time we can note an alliteration in 'w' (whose significance will soon appear), as well as the image of youth with the dreadful marks of old age. Ahasuerus says that, after being cursed by Christ and condemned to endless wanderings on Earth, he fell into a trance:

> But my soul
> From sight and sense of the polluting woe
> Of tyranny, had long learned to prefer
> Hell's freedom to the servitude of Heaven.

[1]'The sweeping storm of Time' (*Op. cit.*, VI, 1.220).

> Therefore I rose, and dauntlessly began
> My lonely and unending pilgrimage,
> Resolved to wage unweariable war
> With my almighty Tyrant...
>
> (VII, ll. 191–198)

The alliteration here follows the related themes of pollution and servitude, which are usually auxiliary to carnivorous, hunter symbols.

In the cosmic description of the same character in *Hellas* (ll. 137–148), wandering is suggested only through the comparison with 'the tempest-sifted snow', the cloud, the winter-wind. Besides, he 'loses his original symbolic force, which had been absorbed by the character of Prometheus (1819), and becomes a type of patient wisdom.'[1]

Therefore it is necessary to search broad contexts and metaphysical presentations in order to find out the wandering-theme connected with Ahasuerus. Baker rightly considers that he is closely modelled on Milton's Satan.[2] Shelley too compares his stoic rebel to a thunderstruck giant oak challenging the storm[3] or to a calm, tall pine. Of course, those are static figures, but one must not be misled by the hieratic appearance: it is an inverted wandering. Instead of the reprobate's endlessly travelling through a tyrannical space, it is time, life, generations, that are ceaselessly whirling around the immobile martyr thus connected with Prometheus bound to his rock. In various passages, the mythical figure of Ahasuerus symbolizes an infernal rambling in space and time, two patterns which are metaphorically united in *Alastor*.

Here, the odyssey is directly suggested by the image of the autumn winds and the dead leaves:

> But the charmed eddies of autumnal winds
> Built o'er his mouldering bones a pyramid
> Of mouldering leaves in the waste wilderness.
>
> (ll. 52–54)

[1] N. I. White, *Shelley* I, p. 653 (New York, A. Knopf, 1940).
[2] C. Baker, *Shelley's Major Poetry*, pp. 277–278 (London, O.U.P., 1948).
[3] See Milton, *Paradise Lost* I, ll. 612–615; Shelley, *Queen Mab*, VII, ll. 259–261.

'Waste wilderness' alone infers the notion of a vain, infinite roaming, and the repetition of 'mouldering', by emphasizing the notion of time, reminds the reader that existence is but a wandering in the night of time. In the next paragraph, the theme takes on a new dimension. It is treated in a rather vague way, stressing the wildness of landscapes ('Many a *wi*de *w*aste and tangled *w*ilderness / Has lured his fearful steps'). The hero is a fabulous hunter in a fantastic setting:

> Nature's most secret steps
> He like her shadow has pursued, where'er
> The red volcano overcanopies
> Its fields of snow and pinnacles of ice
> With burning smoke, or where bitumen lakes
> On black bare pointed islets ever beat
> With sluggish surge, or where the secret caves
> Rugged and dark, winding among the springs
> Of fire and poison, inaccessible
> To avarice and pride, their starry domes
> Of diamond and of gold expand above
> Numberless and immeasurable halls.
>
>   (ll. 81–91)

Those are characteristic landscapes of artistic and mythological reveries: the first picture recalls John Martin's paintings, the second is reminiscent of Stymphalus and the third is in the tradition of cavern literature, in fantastic tales and fairy-tales. The impressive beauty of such scenery is infernal, oppressive, aggressive, due to painful contrasts between the red of the fire, the crude white of the snow, the thick blackness of bituminous lakes, between burning smoke and cold ice. Shapes are predominantly sharp: keen ice, pointed islands; dark, labyrinthine caves, full of fire and poison, are stifling, suggesting a claustrophobia made more perceptible by obsessive alliterations. The landscape itself, in its fixed structures, has the typical characteristics of wearying wanderings, because it unfolds itself as the wanderer discovers it. There follows a happy period crowned by the famous Vision of the Ideal Woman whom the Poet wants to embrace, but it abruptly vanishes (ll. 151–191). He wakes up: 'Whither have fled / The hues of heaven that canopied his bower / Of yesternight?' The poet answers this anxious question by setting off in pursuit of this 'fleeting shade', prompted by a 'desperate hope'. His is the hopeless pursuit of romantic Ideal Beauty dangerously revealed in dream, and never to be granted by reality.

Then his odyssey is obviously turned into a chastisement (ll. 222–271) and Alastor, the evil genius, actually puts in an appearance (ll. 224–227). The distracted hero is compared to the eagle fighting with the snake in the well-known Manichean image. The bird, poisoned by the venom, is a symbol of the poet consumed by his longing for the ideal, his exhausting obsession. The atmosphere is the same as in the first wanderings, the quest becomes a painful flight. The alliteration in 'w' appears again (ll. 242–246), in the words 'waste', 'wild', 'wilderness'; again, in the phrase 'a weary waste of hours' (l. 245), the symbolical dimension asserts itself through the blending of temporal and spatial patterns. And the evolving combination of all those mythical themes leads up to the image of the 'spectral form', like 'the Spirit of the Wind / With lighting eyes, and eager breath and feet / Disturbing not the drifted snow' (ll. 256–261), an obvious evocation of the Wandering Jew in the style of Gustave Doré's illustrations, perhaps inspired by the poet in *Kubla Khan*.

The end of the poem is devoted to nautical wanderings in a threatening setting of toppling rocks, precipices and voracious caves, and leads to a tranquil, serene, regressive death, which is not consistent with the beginning and the preface.

Ahasuerus extends his influence over other wanderers:

> Tell me, thou Star, whose wings of light
> Speed thee in thy fiery flight,
> In what cavern of the night
> Will thy pinions close now?
>
> Tell me, Moon, thou pale and gray
> Pilgrim of Heaven's homeless way,
> In what depth of night or day
> Seekest thou repose now?

Weary wind who wanderest
Like the world's rejected guest
Hast thou still some secret nest
In the tree or billow?[1]

The atmosphere, which is all light and lightness in the first stanza, darkens in the second. Weariness is inferred by 'pale and gray'. An alliteration in 'h' is combined with a repetition of 'w' to which it is sometimes equivalent. The figure of the Wandering Jew looms, to assert itself at the beginning of the third stanza in the image of the wind with the usual alliteration in 'w', and become conspicuous as the background of the phrase 'the world's rejected guest'. The process is the reverse of that of *Alastor*: here the wind is assimilated to Ahasuerus. The two are usually connected in the myth. It is interesting to note the surge of imagination through and above rational data, in the gradual strengthening of an image, rather vague at first, and in the equally gradual and simultaneous emergence of a compelling sensation of weariness which, from the first to the last line, follows the temporal development of the poem itself. Poetic object and poetic intention are rigorously synchronized.

The moon and the ocean itself (strange as it may seem) are also wanderers. And finally, the basic setting of the Shelleyan odyssey is 'life's rough way'[2]; the 'evil wilderness' through which Ahasuerus plods his weary way is man's life on earth. For the great figure is more than legendary: It 'is older than Christianity or even recorded history; its beginnings date back to the time when man first developed a conscience'.[3] It is an archetype, a mythical character made by various artists to embody various values.

Shelley's poetic universe is traversed by other cosmic and natural wanderers with a strong, sombre, unforgettable personality. First, the hosts of dead leaves borne away by autumn winds or streams. They appear in *The Revolt of Islam*, standing for

---

[1] *The World's Wanderers.* Cf. *Fragments of an Unfinished Drama*, II. 4–5, *Poetical Works* (O.U.P.), p. 482.

[2] *Epipsychidion*, I, 72.

[3] J. Gaer, *op. cit.*, p. 152.

clouds (ɪ, iv, ll. 8–9), the great ills of mankind (ɪ, xxix, ll. 1–4), the crowd carried away by an eloquent orator (ɪv, xiii, ll. 8–9 and v, liii, ll. 1–2). And in the tenth canto they are fraught with all their hitherto potential sinister significance:

> Madness, Fear, and Plague, and Famine still
> Heaped corpse on corpse, and as in autumnal woods
> The frosts of many a wind with dead leaves fill
> Earth's cold and sullen brooks . . .
>
> (x, xliv, ll. 2–5)

This image attests the organic unity of the long poem, for the heaped up corpses are those of the men that were carried away by Cythna's eloquence in the fifth canto. Besides, in between, there were two intermediaries, including the following one whose wording will have to be kept in mind:

> There was a desolate village in a wood
> Whose bloom-inwoven leaves now scattering fed
> The hungry storm; . . .
>
> (vɪ, xlvi, ll. 1–3)

During the next three years, the image will remain thoroughly macabre, as in the opening lines of *Ode to the West Wind*:

> Thou from whose unseen presence the leaves dead
> Are driven like ghosts from an enchanter fleeing,
>
> (ll. 2–3)

and then, as an echo, in *The Sensitive Plant*:

> And the leaves, brown, yellow, and gray, and red,
> And white, with the whiteness of what is dead,
> Like troops of ghosts on the dry wind passed,
>
> (ɪɪɪ, ll. 34–36)

Our great mythical figure obviously looms again in the imaginal background of the dark hosts which seem temporarily to outlive their day in those ghostly flights. The reader cannot miss the essential elements of the customary setting: darkness, tempest, whistling wind, a tragic atmosphere, an impression of weariness or resignation, the torturing alliance of life and death, tearing away and wandering, plus our alliteration which covers the whole stanza of *The Sensitive Plant*. This is a real modulation of the Ahasuerus theme, a splitting up of the character.

The other striking image is that of clouds. They often symbolize Shelley's longing for divine liberty, and actualize a recurrent fundamental, paradisiac dream with a classical significance.[1] But in a famous poem of 1816, combining flight and agitation, they are emblems of mutability,[2] a cause of romantic pathos since it is related to the time obsession and condemns all living creatures—like the plastic cloud—to a torturing evolution. One of the most pathetic representations of this situation is the hoary-haired young man wondering at his own reflection in water. The first approach in *Alastor* (written in the same year as *Mutability*) breaks the hero's wanderings.[3] The image reappears in the first canto of *The Revolt of Islam*:

> A dying poet gave me books and blessed
> With wild but holy talk, the sweet unrest
> In which I watched him as he died away—
> A youth with hoary hair—a fleeting guest
> Of our lone mountains: . . .
>
> (I, xxxvii, ll. 4–8)

The irreversible dynamism of passing life is substituted for the reflection in water, with the same significance. Then:

> I saw my countenance reflected there;—
> And when my youth fell on me like a wind
> Descending on still waters—my thin hair
> Was prematurely gray, my face was lined

---

[1] See Jean Perrin, *Les Structures de l'imaginaire shelleyen* (Grenoble, 1973), pp. 578–594. (Presses Universitaires de Grenoble, 1973).

[2] See *Mutability*, II. 1–4.

[3] See *Alastor*, II, 469–474.

> With channels, such as suffering leaves behind,
> Not age; my brow was pale, but in my cheek
> And lips a flush of gnawing fire did find
> Their food and dwelling . . .
>
> (IV, xxix, ll. 1–8)

The image recurs in *Lines* (*Nov. 5th 1817*), *Death, Rosalind and Helen* (v. 151). Its constellation is remarkably constant: hair, darkness, water, with a patent suggestion of elapsing time. It bears out Gilbert Durand's definition of 'the black water constellation' in *Les Structures Anthropologiques de l'Imaginaire* and provides an exact illustration of his commentary[1]: running water, in *Lines* (ll. 8–9) symbolizes Heraclitean time, and a typical 'ophelization' is performed in the dark depths which reflect Laon and the Poet of *Alastor*, an explicit representation of the dark realm of a near death already harbouring the aging image of the young hero.

In *Prometheus Unbound*, man's predicament is conveyed by the capital image of the deer chased by the pack of hungry Hours (IV, ll. 73–76), to which most of those mentioned so far ineluctably led (as the symbolical impersonation of an important aspect of Shelley's psyche). Its analogy with *Alastor* is obvious in that it also blends time and space in the same thematic patterns. It even helps in understanding that poem. The hunter-hero, scouring the world in pursuit of his ideal, is a hunted quarry in fact. Several details show it: 'he eagerly pursues / Beyond the realm of dream, that fleeting shade' (ll. 205–206); then, after quiet days:

> At night the passion came
> Like the fierce fiend of a distempered dream,
> And shook him from his rest, and led him forth
> Into the darkness.
>
> (ll. 225–227)

Next comes the image in which he is compared to the eagle entwined with the serpent, and the portrait that likens him with the Wandering Jew. The Poet is hunted down by the fierce demon of

[1] Presses Universitaires de France, 1963, p. 93. *et seq.*

his dreams. 'To flee' is used thirteen times in the poem. After gazing at his aging face in the still water of a fountain, he sets off again toward a quiet death, an indirect victim of the pack of fierce hounds called desires, cravings, frustrations.

In *The Cenci*, the tortured lover is relentlessly pursued by the image of the beloved.[1]

The synthetic picture of man—and of the author—to be derived from the three excerpts above is that of a fleeing, hunted, distracted victim.

After another development in *Letter to Maria Gisborne* (ll. 187–192), this image emerges again in *Epipsychidion*, as a definitive synthesis applied to the author:

> In many mortal forms I rashly sought
> The Shadow of that idol of my thought . . .
> Then as a hunted deer that could not flee,
> I turned upon my thoughts, and stood at bay,
> Wounded, and weak, and panting; the cold day
> Trembled, for pity of my strife and pain.
>
> (ll. 267–8, 272–5)

The last line but one recalls the famous line of *Ode to the West Wind*:

> I fall upon the thorns of life, I bleed!

which was so strongly criticized by representatives of the New Criticism, and in which the thorn is a surrogate for animal fangs.

We have obviously to deal not only with a recurring image, but with a 'personal myth', with a real obsession, so constant and consistent, so conspicuous for the analyst, that for years it must have haunted the unconscious of its creator. It seems to have the typical characteristics of a complex (as C. G. Jung defines it) which, after a protracted gestation, is born at last to the author's

[1]   Because I am a Priest, do you believe
            Your image, as the hunter some struck deer,
            Follows me not whether I wake or sleep?
                                    (I, ii, ll. 11–13)

consciousness, and fully reveals itself in *Adonais*, in which Shelley
bemoans Keats's death, while thinking of himself:

> Midst others of less note, came one frail Form,
> A phantom among men; companionless
> As the last cloud of an expiring storm
> Whose thunder is its knell; he as I guess,
> Had gazed on Nature's naked loveliness
> Actaeon-like, and now he fled astray
> With feeble steps o'er the world's wilderness,
> And his own thoughts, along that rugged way
> Pursued, like raging hounds, their father and their prey.
>
> (xxxi)

Now we know what the myth is, and I suggest calling the complex it represents the Actaeon complex.

The image of *Adonais* is extremely interesting, for, as often
happens in Shelley, it is a thorough synthesis and the outcome of a
long development, a long maturing in the depths of the poetic
unconscious. Is it not, among other things, an exact epitome of the
Alastor situation in psycho-mythological terms? Like Adonais, the
Poet of *Alastor* was unwittingly rash enough, in an ecstasy, to
contemplate Ideal Beauty, an unveiled Artemis, jealous of her own
perfection, who cannot accept being beheld with impunity. Then
it is that the hunter becomes a quarry and that his thoughts turn
against him, like Actaeon's hounds when he is changed into a
stag, and compel him to pathetic, hopeless wanderings, which
are both a useless quest of the Vision and a flight from the unbearable void left by the dream in everyday life. It is an aspect of
Platonic love: Eros, the son of Penia (Want). The visionary poet's
predicament is similar to that of the addict, another being hunted
down by an inner need. All Shelley's great poems, of course, are
more or less consciously autobiographical: if 'companionless' is
reminiscent of the Sensitive Plant, a static image of its own creator, the main elements of the stanza under consideration recall
Ahasuerus to whom the young Shelley assimilated himself: the
frail, strong being, the 'phantom among men',[1] the wind, the

---

[1] 'His inessential figure cast no shade' (*Queen Mab*, VII, l. 71).

cloud, the storm, the rumbling thunder, the flight along life's interminable rugged path, and naturally the alliteration in the seventh line.

The image of the hunted deer will be used again in *Adonais*,[1] and the definite emergence of the Actaeon myth here sheds a new light on a certain number of elements that were endowed earlier with a potential symbolic value.

The theme of mangled flesh was already present in the sixth canto of *Queen Mab*, in the image of the thorns combined with that of the demon and his prey, followed by that of the chain, also an aspect of the mastication theme in Shelley,[2] and that of the scorpion, which stings itself to death (VI, ll. 36–38). The pointed shapes of hellish landscapes in *Alastor* now appear as fangs threatening the wanderer, the 'rugged' caverns yawn like carnivorous mouths (ll. 83–88), and when Shelley writes:

> The crags closed round with black and jaggèd arms,
> The shattered mountains overhung the sea,
> ....
> ....A cavern there
> Yawned and amid its slant and winding depths
> Ingulfed the rushing sea . . .
>
> (ll. 359–365)

we realize that the closing jagged arms are jaws indeed. Such is the usual suggestion of 'jagged', not only in such expressions as 'the jaggèd alligator'[3] or 'the jaggèd-jawèd lion'[4] which inevitably affect all other uses of the term, but also in the descriptions of the 'jaggèd gulf' of the sea which swallows ships.[5] The image appears twice in *The Revolt of Islam*: in the 'jaggèd caverns' of canto XII (xix, l. 6) and especially in the description of the 'jaggèd islets' surrounded by the ocean gulf, which Laon beholds from a graveyard surrounded with tombs (II, x). Later on, the *Alastor*

---

[1] 'A herd-abandoned deer struck by the hunter's dart' (xxxiii, l. 9).
[2] *Queen Mab*, VI, l. 28, p. 783. See Jean Perrin, *op. cit.*, pp. 295, 387.
[3] *Prometheus Unbound*, IV, l. 309.
[4] *Homer's Hymn to Mercury*, l. 757.
[5] *Queen Mab*, IV, ll. 30–33.

Poet penetrates into a forest, a world of harmony (ll. 420–459)
where the reader is reminded of Alastor's perpetual threat only
by 'huge caves / Scooped in the dark base of their aëry rocks',
which 'respond and roar for ever' (ll. 423–425). We cannot but
note, after Gilbert Durand, the close symbolic connection between the animal's roar and carnivorous voracity.[1] All those
images and unconscious suggestions lead up to the description of
the scenery just before the Poet dies, which confirms our hypo-
thesis of a fang obsession:

> On every side now rose
> Rocks, which, in unimaginable forms,
> Lifted their black and barren pinnacles
> In the light of evening, and, its precipice
> Obscuring the ravine, disclosed above
> Mid toppling stones, black gulfs and yawning caves,
> Whose windings gave ten thousand various tongues
> To the loud stream. Lo! where the pass expands
> Its stony jaws, the abrupt mountain breaks . . .
>
> (ll. 543–553)

This is indeed a synthesis, made clear by the phrase 'stony jaws',
of all the elements noted above: black, barren pinnacles, islets,
yawning, roaring caverns. The theme of mineral mastication,
supported by a rugged consonantal dominant, is linked with the
swallowing scheme, especially at the end of the paragraph:

> whilst the broad river,
> Foaming and hurrying o'er its rugged path,
> Fell into that *immeasurable void*.
>
> (italics mine)

This analysis shows the early presence of the Actaeon complex in
Shelley's poetry and psyche. The wanderer is perturbed by the
fang obsession, and the developments of the two themes reach a
final climax at the same time, just before the death of the hero, at
the very moment when the jaw image unambiguously emerges
from the various symbolical surrogates found earlier.

[1] Gilbert Durand, *op. cit.*, p. 80.

The complex is also revealed by a close analysis of the above-mentioned images of *The Revolt of Islam*: 'inwoven leaves ... *fed | The hungry storm*', and when the poet writes that 'The frosts of many a wind with dead leaves fills | Earth's cold and sullen brooks', we are reminded of the 'northern wind, wandering about | Like a wolf' in *The Sensitive Plant*, at the end of which winter is compared first to a riding huntsman with a pack of hounds, and then to a solitary wolf (two images which are undeniably related to the Actaeon myth), while the cold rain falling from the clouds meets the icy dew rising from the ground, like two closing frost jaws (ll. 102–105). To return to *The Revolt of Islam*, it is evidently suggested that the fleeting hosts of dead leaves are swallowed up into the yawning mouth of time, like the clouds. And is not the hoary-haired young man (a 'fleeting guest'), in whose 'cheek | And lips a flush of *gnawing fire* did find | Their food and dwelling' (a wraith in fact), symbolically swallowed into the Element which symbolizes rolling time?

Therefore the fang is an element of the great, heroic dualism in Shelley's poetry: in the omnipresent symbolic contest of the wing and the chain (most obviously imaged by the snake and the eagle wreathed in struggle), it associates with the chain. Already in *The Daemon of the World*, the serpent's coil is equivalent to ruthless jaws 'crushing the bones of some frail antilope', the animal which is presented, in a beautiful image of *Epipsychidion*, as the lightest and most Shelleyan of quadrupeds (ll. 75–77). Indeed, the Actaeon complex surreptitiously animates *Epipsychidion* too:

> At length into the obscure Forest came
> The Vision I had sought through grief and shame.
> Athwart that wintry wilderness of thorns
> Flashed from her motion splendour like the Morn's.
> (ll. 321–324)

There are no hounds, but thorns tear, and this Vision will actually induce an unbearable want, until the poet ejaculates:

> I pant, I sink, I tremble, I expire!

which might well be a description of the dying stag brought to bay.

The figure of Christ with his crown of thorns also appears twice in *Hellas* and *Prometheus Unbound*.[1] This torture, symbolically related to the treatment inflicted on Orpheus by the Maenads, also shows, it seems, a liberation of sadistic (manducatory) tendencies. The hero of *Alastor* is unquestionably akin to Orpheus, the Poet who is hunted down and mangled to death. An analysis of Shelley's *Orpheus* reveals the same obsession expressed by the same elements in the setting: a 'pointed hill, / Crowned with a ring of oaks' (ll. 1–2); near this 'jagged and shapeless hill' (l. 18) yawns a cave (l. 19). Then a 'mighty cataract . . . casts itself with horrid roar and din' (l. 74), while, incidentally, to describe the heart-rending effect of the desperate song, Shelley compares it to 'A fierce south blast *tear(ing)* through the darkened sky' (l. 88). The obsession thus diluted in the general setting crystallizes in the following lines:

> As a poor hunted stag
> A moment shudders on the fearful brink
> Of a swift stream—the cruel hounds press on
> With deafening yell, the arrows glance and wound,
> He plunges in: so Orpheus, seized and torn
> By the sharp fangs of an insatiate grief,
> Maenad-like waved his lyre in the bright air.
>
> (ll. 46–52)

Would it be irrelevant to suggest, as a background, the picture of Harriet at bay on the brink of the Serpentine a few years before? It is certainly not irrelevant, at any rate, to assimilate the writer to Orpheus: a most musical poet pursued by disappointments and griefs. The myth of Orpheus, of the poet who cannot live without his creative imagination, who is led by his passion to the heart of forbidden mysteries, who falls a prey to ideal feminine beauty and is hunted down and torn to pieces, is not unlike the Actaeon myth.

The latter underlies almost all Shelley's great poems, including

---

[1] *Prometheus Unbound*, i, l. 598; *Prol. Hellas*, l. 122.

Prometheus Unbound (especially in the image of the Furies, those sinister creatures begot by the very personality of the hero, gnashing their metallic teeth and torturing their creator). Present (and concealed) from the start in the myth of the Wandering Jew, it is then clearly superimposed on it, to develop later into the Orpheus myth. But if the dominants come in succession, and reveal a growing awareness of the poet, the inevitable diachrony in the act of writing, which compels me to quote them successively, may be a source of error, because in fact the three cohabit from the start, though the Actaeon myth will prevail. One can even speak of four myths, since Shelley's Prometheus, an Actaeon too (though a static one), is only a modulation of his Ahasuerus.

A close analysis of Shelleyan symbolism and mythology shows that, in conformity with the fundamental nature of mythology and symbolism, they have several simultaneous meanings, at various levels. Two movements are to be discerned, with two opposite poles: an infernal constellation of paralysis, captivity, flight, dominated by the Father image, including a number of significant themes: chain, fang, tyrant, gold, blood, victims (flowers, leaves, worm, fawn, deer, stag, antilope), hunters (hounds, wolves, Furies, vultures), minerals, night, death, madness, Jupiter, Prometheus, Cenci, Ahasuerus, Orpheus and the Actaeon myth; and a regressive constellation dominated by the Mother image, with all the symbols of happy nestling (flowers, cavern, forest, sea etc.), cradled escape (flying, sailing), harmony and Venus.

The prevalence of the wanderer theme and the Actaeon myth in Shelley can be accounted for biographically (in the narrow sense of the word). We know that at the age of 19, when he was expelled from Oxford for proclaiming his atheism, Shelley broke with his father to spend the rest of his life as a wanderer. Penniless, he lived on post-obits, ran into debts which he could not pay off, and had to escape creditors, frequently changing houses. At the same time, he assumed the responsibility of the debts contracted by his father-in-law (and intellectual ideal), William Godwin, whom he managed to relieve more than a little. And, to crown all, on February 28th 1815, Doctor Pemberton warned him that abscesses were forming on his lungs and that he was rapidly dying of consumption. Later, in Italy, suffering no longer from his lungs but from a terrible pain in his side, having lost several of his nearest friends and relatives (including Mary's two children), he complained of being literally hunted down by death. Before that, back from Ireland with Harriet, having noticed that the police kept an eye on his activities—and his mail—he thought—and I believe he *felt*—he was being pursued, an obsession which was to reach its climax in the famous, still mysterious Tann y R'allt aggression. And I shall simply recall in passing the incident told by Hogg: during a walk he was taking with Shelley, just before their expulsion from Oxford, the latter was attacked by an over-zealous watch-dog which he got rid of with great difficulty, at the cost of his coat-tails. Young Bysshe, who was usually so mild, flew into a rage, and Hogg had a hard time preventing him from shooting the dog with his pistols. In my analysis of *Alastor* and *Epipsychidion*, I have dealt with the spiritual meaning of the Actaeon myth, which symbolizes the idealist and his torments. Finally, from the more general point of view of neo-platonic metaphysics (which influenced much of Shelley's work and *Prometheus Unbound* more particularly), those endless wanderings on life's rough way are the consequence of individuation and the loss of harmony which every soul desperately seeks to recover.

This shows the capital importance of myths as revelatory, and, at the same time, symbolic images of the self, as forces giving shape to biographical and spiritual experience. For the Actaeon complex, progressively emerging from the Wandering Jew image (in which it was in fact already included, since Ahasuerus is ever *pursued* by divine revenge, a consequence of his own sin), has appeared as a self-representation (unconscious at first, and then growing more and more conscious). Biographical data provided important clues to this 'personal myth'. But we must not forget that Shelley's interest in the Wandering Jew dates back to his years of adolescence—before the events recounted. It seems, therefore, that the primordial myth informed the poet's exis-tence, that he conformed, as the outcome of an inner determinism, to the symbolical picture of himself provided by mythology. This is quite congruent with the findings of modern psychoanalytical research. Of course, this type of penetration into the unconscious, necessary as it is, may sometimes appear dubious and dangerous. It is the price to be paid for man's will to know more about himself.

IV

Lever's 'Lord Kilgobbin'

A. NORMAN JEFFARES

CHARLES LEVER has been unreasonably treated by most critics of Anglo-Irish literature. He wrote thirty-three novels in thirty-five years, between 1837 and 1872, and these are not at all the same in tone. Lever, however, has been generally dismissed by Irish critics as a novelist who dealt in stage Irish characters or merely gave a picture of the lighter side of garrison life in Ireland. The labels rightly attached to his earlier novels *Harry Lorrequer* (1837), *Charles O'Malley* (1841) and *Arthur O'Leary* (1844) were also applied to his subsequent and very different novels. The earlier novels, light-hearted and full of lively incident, were rollicking romps of nineteenth-century gaiety, akin most of all perhaps in their ebullience to the farcical elements in Farquhar's earlier comedies. Carleton attacked Lever, notably in an unsigned review in *The Nation*, October 1843, in which he accused Lever of 'selling us for pounds, shillings and pence', and regarded him as not unlike a common informer 'receiving good pay from England for bearing false witness against his country'. Political leaders also criticized him adversely, Daniel O'Connell with some savagery and Thomas Davis with a dislike of his 'Donnybrook school' depictions of Irishmen. When Lever left Ireland in 1845, the attacks largely ceased. Lever himself had begun to write historical rather than military novels, to examine the social milieu outside Ireland in European novels, to take in the political scene and to comment critically on life itself.

This deepening in Lever's understanding, accompanied as it was by corresponding developments in style and technique, seems not to have been acknowledged by critics in Ireland. It was as if the earlier nationalistic commentators had precluded any subsequent detachment of viewpoint, any objective analysis of what Lever was actually writing from the middle of the 'forties to the middle 'fifties, or indeed as if they had created a climate in which barely any comment at all was made on his writings after 1845. From the middle eighteen-fifties to his last novel *Lord Kilgobbin* (1872) Lever wrote several novels which might well have appealed even to extremely nationalistic critics: but the labels had been printed in the 'thirties and 'forties and continued to be attached. There was one perceptive article in *Blackwood's Magazine*, April 1862, which, while it mourned the departure of the earlier heroes, did recognize Lever's increased novelistic skill and deeper human sympathy.

Yeats, however, continued the denigration. Intent on rooting out from Irish literature the image of the stage Irishman, he entirely failed to do justice to Lever's later novels, let alone the earlier. One is driven to speculate on whether he had ever read, say, *Barrington* (1863), *Sir Brook Fossbrooke* (1866), or *Lord Kilgobbin* (1872). E. A. Boyd followed Yeats's example, stressing the stage Irish element in Lever in *Ireland's Literary Renaissance* (1968). Stephen Gwynn and Hugh Law, however, realized that Lever had been unreasonably denigrated, but Daniel Corkery naturally enough found Lever unacceptable in his view of Anglo-Irish literature. Contemporary critics tend to follow these traditional views, Benedict Kiely, for instance, stressing the rollicking aspect of Lever's work in *Modern Irish Fiction* (1950) while Thomas Flanagan excludes him (as he does Maturin) from consideration in *The Irish Novel, 1800–1850* (1959) and Vivian Mercier in *The Irish Comic Tradition* (1962) concentrates on Lever's small development of the grotesque. There are some exceptions. For instance, Roger McHugh in 'Charles Lever', an article in *Studies* XXVII, 1938, argued that Lever gave a full picture of various aspects of political and social life in nineteenth-century Ireland, and it is significant that Shaw had earlier acknowledged his debt to Lever in the preface to *Major Barbara* (1905). He found Lever poignant, and Lever's tragi-comic treatment of the irony of the conflict between real life and the romantic imagination as well as the earlier writer's impartiality impressed him deeply.

This detached impartiality grew steadily in Lever and reached its fullest development in his last novel *Lord Kilgobbin*. This novel, written between 1870 and 1872, was dedicated to the memory of his wife, and written 'in breaking health and broken spirits'. In it Lever casts a cold eye on political life in both Ireland and England; analytically aware of the interactions between the two countries, he shows that he had learned—probably from Maria Edgeworth and from Disraeli's political novels—the attraction of blending political affairs with those of the heart. His novel is no romance; the common sense materialism of marriage looms large in the thoughts if not always the emotions of its younger as well as its older characters.

Lord Kilgobbin is a long novel, of about 220,000 words, and it moves, at first, at a leisurely pace. Its tempo, however, quickens considerably as the story progresses, its complications develop and its interest intensifies. This is a sombre book. Lever sets most of the action in the flat midland country of Ireland, Kilgobbin Castle being situated in King's County (modern Offaly) and near to Moate, in present-day Westmeath. The rain is early described as falling steadily on the bogland and through its pervading presence Lever evokes the smell of damp decay which invests the whole Irish situation in his day. The landlords were decadent—indeed the Kilgobbin estate is no model of management, and evictions, inevitably the cause of much human suffering, take place on a neighbouring estate—yet while Lever dislikes the manner in which the British government is ruling Ireland he is equally distrustful of the apparent alternative of mob rule which a successful Fenian rising might introduce. The future is unsettled and decidedly disturbing.

Against this background Lever gives us the drama of his plot. He owed much to Scott. Like Scott he can lapse into blank verse in his narrative descriptions; like Scott he can prolong the earlier stages of a story to what becomes, for modern readers, a tediously drawn out length; but like Scott he can create unusual characters and create an evocative regional atmosphere. He also owed much to Balzac, and he presents us in this novel with a Balzacian view of life. Confidently in control of his canvas, he writes with the skill and control of experience, and he has an eye for significant detail, for dialogue, and for the general Irish social scene.

Lever focusses interest on the eighty younger characters. To a certain extent he may have been influenced by Maria Edgeworth's novel *Patronage* (1814), in which she discussed the problem of how members of an Anglo-Irish family were to make their way in the world—a matter obviously discussed frequently and fully in the talkative Edgeworth family, for Maria's father Richard Lovell Edgeworth had had twenty-two children by his four wives. Lever shows us two undergraduates at Trinity College who have not yet settled on suitable careers. Dick Kearney, the son of the owner of Kilgobbin Castle, echoes his father's earlier extravagances. He is slow, plodding, self-satisfied and dull: in short not a very attractive young man. Lever contrasts him with Joseph Atlee, who shares his rooms in college. The son of a Presbyterian minister in Northern Ireland, Atlee is indolent, discursive, superficial and decidedly sharp-witted. Irresistibly attracted by the fraudulent in literature, he himself writes anonymously for journals of different political beliefs as well as secretly writing nationalist ballads. Something of his ambitious nature appears in the soliloquies which Lever supplies as an occasional change from his own role as omniscient narrator, and in an early piece of self-communing Atlee also ponders on the contrast between his intellectual powers and his penniless state. During the course of the novel we trace Dick's emergence from self-satisfaction into annoyance at his father's idea of a career in law for him; he has no interest in the estate and forms a plan of emigrating to Australia: finally he is given a place in the police, through Atlee's not entirely disinterested efforts. Atlee's own career is pursued with energy and skill, once he has seen a way into the world of affairs through making himself useful to the Viceroy's aide-de-camp, Cecil Walpole, and later to the Viceroy himself, Lord Danesbury.

Dick Kearney and Joseph Atlee are young Irishmen in search of a career. It is perhaps significant that they are contrasted with two practical and pragmatic young Englishmen both already successfully launched into theirs. Cecil Walpole, a gifted dilettante, greater in promise than performance, has done a little of almost everything and likes to display 'the scores of things he might be, instead of that mild very ordinary young gentleman' that he is. A promising Whig, he is summed up by Lever as a political animal, who coquets with Radical views but fastidiously avoids contact with the mob. (Lever had been disillusioned by Whiggery, and his dislike of Gladstone shines through at times, not least in the matter of the weaker clarets.) We meet him in the Blue Goat at Moate, where he and his companion have come on a fishing trip from Dublin. His friend, Major Henry Lockwood, another aide-de-camp, takes a Wellingtonian view of the need for 'putting down': a good soldier, a 'very safe' character, his dullness is similar to Dick Kearney's, though we discover later that he is unlike Dick in being proud of his estate in England, which, though small, is very successfully run. Something of Scott's puzzlement at how the English are more successful than the Scots underlies Lever's presentation of these four young men: why are the English more *au fait* with the ways of the world than the Irishmen; why should they possess power while the equally intelligent, more lively and imaginative Irish do not? He concentrates attention on the two more intelligent young men: the successful English politician and the Irish would-be politician; we see Atlee's fortunes rising as Walpole's fall. Both men pursue the same two women with some calculation and these involvements form a lively part of the latter stages of the novel.

Lever often gave his women characters more life and energy, more force of personality than his men, and in *Lord Kilgobbin* he drew yet another contrast: between Kate Kearney, who managed her father's estate, insofar as it could be managed, with the Stewart, Peter Gill, as a kind of Grand Vizier. Her 'fine temper and genial disposition' offset Gill's craft and subtlety in dealing with the tenants, who are wretchedly poor (but, as Lever is careful to point out, far from unhappy). Kate is unambitious and unpretentious; an open-air girl, she likes living at Kilgobbin. This is a difficult experience for her cousin Nina Kostalergi, who has recently arrived at the Castle and finds its lack of social life very different from the fashionable world she has known in Italy. Her mother, Matthew Kearney's sister, had married the Secretary of the Greek legation at Naples, Spiridion Kostalergi, a compulsive gambler who lost his post after a duel. This was a romantic

marriage—the Irish girl having earlier refused 'sensible offers'—
but after Nina's mother had died in poverty in Palermo Spiridion
brought Nina to Rome intending to make her a *prima donna*. She
has escaped this fate by fleeing to Ireland and appealing to
Matthew who takes her into the family. She sings superbly, she
paints, she converses well and she is highly temperamental and
flirtatious. Lever provides a steady view of the realities of marriage
both in his own comments and in the conversations of the characters throughout the novel: social position and financial standing
are carefully considered by the characters though emotion will
keep breaking through!

The two girls receive Walpole at the Castle in Matthew's
absence—Lockwood has disapproved of the visit once he hears
Walpole had known Nina in Italy, for Walpole is engaged to his
cousin Lady Maude Bickerstaffe—and Walpole anticipates some
romantic episode as he is driven across the wet bogland from
Moate to the Castle. A very different kind of episode, however,
ensues, for the Castle is attacked by an armed band in search of
weapons. Kate is largely responsible for a successful defence of the
Castle against them, and in this affray Walpole is wounded. Nina
teases him about his declaration to her in Italy, and she quickly sees
through Atlee's ambitions (he and Dick have arrived at the Castle
after the affray) and tells him that he and she are both Bohemians.

Lever varies the action and skilfully threads his characters in
and out of the plot. Matthew Kearney has been described as an
indolent and impoverished landlord. He is known locally as
Lord Kilgobbin (James the Second had created an ancestor a
viscount; he had sheltered the fleeing king after the Battle of the
Boyne, but the title was largely concealed during the Williamite
period). His eccentric neighbour Betty O'Shea visits him and
reveals that Peter Gill who has resigned will become her Stewart
at Shea's Barn. She is no respecter of persons, her direct speech is
overbearing, and she is unreasonable, indeed, unfair, in her treatment of Kate. She is determined her nephew Gorman O'Shea, now
serving in the Austrian army, shall form no connection with the
improvident Kearneys. Nina, with justification, calls her 'an in-
sufferable old woman.'

Two more men enter the story. While Atlee is making himself agreeable to Walpole and later to the Viceroy in Wales, Dick Kearney finds Atlee's friend Dan Donoghan in his rooms at Trinity, and invites him to stay *incognito* at the Castle. He persuades Dick to stand as a candidate for King's County. Donoghan is a Fenian leader who has escaped from Dartmoor. Gorman O'Shea returns on leave from Austria to visit his aunt. His return coincides with a political meeting at Moate. Lever gives us an acute analysis of the political situation from Donoghan's point of view as well as the line pursued by the local Whig candidate, who dines with Miss O'Shea and enlists support from the Catholic Church.

Lever's earlier novels favoured military heroes and in *Lord Kilgobbin* the two more dashing characters win the ladies, after overcoming apparently insuperable difficulties. Gorman O'Shea is cut off by his aunt, and given hospitality by Matthew while he makes up his mind what to do. He has not sufficient funds to supplement his pay in the Austrian army. He becomes involved in a misunderstanding with Peter Gill which leads to both of them falling out of a balcony at Shea's Barn, whereupon Gill's supporters beat up O'Shea savagely. Though he eventually recovers he has to be hurried from the gaol to Kilgobbin Castle (a nice piece of co-operation between Matthew Kearney and the Tory magistrates) only to face the threat of charges of burglary and assault— O'Shea not having realized his aunt had virtually handed over her estate to Gill. Donoghan meanwhile has declared his romantic interest in Nina, but he is on the run, and she is likely to marry Walpole who, after Lady Maude has broken with him, proposes to Nina and is accepted on condition his family receive her. By this time his plans to avoid confrontation with the Fenians have become public property whereupon Lord Danesbury has resigned as Viceroy. Walpole has been appointed Ambassador to Guatemala—an undistinguished and dangerous post—Lord Danesbury taking up his old post as Ambassador to the Porte.

Atlee, whose insinuations have helped to increase the breach between Walpole and Lady Maude, himself makes a declaration to this cold English beauty and, repulsed, thinks of marrying Nina. He has gone to Turkey and Greece on Lord Danesbury's business and has almost negotiated a payment of £10,000 from Lord Danesbury to Spiridion Kostalergi (for the return of indiscreet letters) which is to be Nina's dowry. But he fails in virtually all his plans. Nina, who has been conveying information to Donoghan about the measures taken against him and also telling him that some of those through whom, he had told her, messages could be secretly conveyed to him, were informers, finally runs away with him, being married in Maryborough on their way to a new life in America. Donoghan has ordered Peter Gill and other witnesses to leave Ireland, so the case against O'Shea collapses. His aunt, moved by his illness, returns to arrange his becoming master of Shea's Barn and the estate on condition he marries Kate, who has earlier refused a lamely put proposal from Lockwood. Atlee conveys the news of Nina's marriage to Walpole who—not unreasonably, given his nature—finds it all very Irish.

Any résumé of the plot of this novel hardly reveals the total effect of its portrayal of a county torn with unrest. Lever mocks the Viceregal system, officialdom's government of Ireland from Dublin Castle. Lord Danesbury (who is a Disraelian character) is appointed because he knows nothing of Ireland, and, once he has performed some official duties, retreats to his family place in Wales, still interested in the affairs of Turkey where he had previously been ambassador. He leaves everything in Ireland to subordinates whose methods are to divide and rule. Lever's satiric exposé of Castle policies follows on the earlier attack in *Sir Brook Fossbrooke* (1866) where he expressed his unease at the methods of government. He is, of course, equally ready to reveal the inefficiencies and unreliability of the Fenian movement, notoriously riddled by intelligence agents and informers paid by Dublin Castle. Donoghan realizes that he is out of step with the times and has the intelligence to leave Ireland.

The movement from the corruption or the decadence of the landlord to the emergence into power of a new commercial middle-class from the peasantry is hinted at in the career of Peter Gill. This is yet another echo, perhaps, of Maria Edgeworth. In *Castle Rackrent* the process takes place with four generations of Rackrents and two of the Quirkes, for Thady, the apparently loyal stewart of the Rackrent family, tells the story of how the estate is finally taken over by his son Jason. Peter Gill goes through the whole cycle himself, for he begins as an apparently loyal stewart to the Kearneys, then reveals his tougher nature in arranging the evictions on the Shea's Barn Estate, next becomes an unscrupulous user of the law in trying to retain his hold on Shea's Barn (which has only been leased to him by Betty O'Shea for a year for a nominal sum) and then is ready to give false evidence against Gorman O'Shea before he is banished by Donoghan's decree.

So Gorman O'Shea inherits his estate, and marries Kate, and Donoghan heads for success in America with Nina as his wife. The would-be politicians, Walpole and Atlee, do not receive the rewards for which they schemed, Dick Kearney and Henry Lockwood will remain dull (Betty O'Shea's Irish denunciation of the latter's English dullness being an intensification of Atlee's earlier musings), Lady Maude will no doubt continue on her cold-blooded courses, and the problem of Ireland will certainly remain.

Lever reveals himself as truly Anglo-Irish in this novel. He enjoys character—the minor episodes, such as Matthew Kearney's row with the Goat Club and the visit of the Dublin specialists to Kilgobbin to treat Gorman O'Shea, are well done—and he analyses the differences between English and Irish sensibilities well, not least in his disquisition on Irish chaffing or teasing. He likes Ireland itself, rain and all, and he despairs of extreme solutions. He has come a long way from his early establishment views. The British party system was at fault. Westminster, he concludes, is no substitute for a parliament in College Green. Indeed Lever had finally moved to a desire for home rule, and *Lord Kilgobbin* explains why he thought it necessary. His political comments throughout the novel are shrewd and they carry weight because he conveys them with the appearance of a certain sardonic detachment. His social comments are often warmer: he can capture a lively conversation; he conveys the atmosphere of a drawing room or a dining room with skill. One of the pleasantest of the novel's incidents is the meeting between Kearney and the Tory magistrate and the local rector where orange and green unite in order to achieve the humane purpose of getting Gorman O'Shea out of danger (Lever's penchant for describing good food and wine pervades most of his novels). He has, however, few illusions about Ireland: he paints the incompetence of the Fenians clearly and he shows the venial informers at their work, and he cannot resist some comic scenes at the expense of the local Chief Constable whose men seize Walpole's luggage and papers, with grave results, when searching the Castle for traces of Donoghan.

He records vanity and wit and he also succeeds in conveying a natural and likeable virtue in Kate. His range of characters is wide: here he particularly shows the influence of Balzac, whom he greatly admired. As always he is shrewd in observing national characteristics. Thus we have frequent illustrations of Irish persiflage; we have Irish comment on such aberrations of English rule as the famine relief works—Walpole finds a road ends in the midst of the Bog of Allen and is told:

> It's one of their tricks the English played on us in the year of the famine. They got two millions of money to make roads in Ireland, but they were so afraid it would make us prosperous and richer than themselves, that they set about making roads that go nowhere. Sometimes to the top of a mountain, or down to the sea, where there was no harbour, and sometimes like this one, into the heart of a bog.

Here are the views of Molyneux and Swift all over again about English economic exploitation of Ireland, and Lever, too, felt fierce indignation at the English politicians who vacillated between repression and submission to terrorism, with the result that Ireland's problems multiplied, the secret societies flourished and divided a population weakened by the effects of the famine and subsequent emigration. Ireland was in his view uneasy, disquieted and angry. He described himself, in April 1871, during his last visit to England and Ireland from Trieste where he was British Consul, as half mad between gout and indignation. But Gladstone at Whitby was worse than his swollen ankle, and he had come to dislike and distrust English rule while realising that the Anglo-Irish ascendancy's power had long vanished. No wonder his last days were haunted, as a reviewer wrote of *Lord Kilgobbin* in the *Dublin University Magazine*, July 1872, 'with a melancholy and over-true foreboding of great catastrophe'. He had moved from comedy through elements of tragi-comedy to a tragic view of life in the Ireland he loved.

V

The Wandering Rocks, or the Rejection of Stephen Dedalus

GIORGIO MELCHIORI

IN an admirable lecture on 'Joyce and Stephen Dedalus', Seamus Deane put very forcibly the case for seeing a continuous process at work throughout Joyce's writings up to and including *Ulysses*—a process of abolition of Stephen Dedalus, a progressive break between the artist and society, so that *Ulysses* marks, in his own words, 'the purgation of society from the novel'. The same view was put in different terms by Raymond Williams when, in considering Joyce's representation of the city, he wrote:

> The genius of *Ulysses* is that it dramatizes three forms of consciousness (and in this sense three characters)—Bloom, Stephen and Molly. Their interaction but also their lack of connection is the tension of composition of the city itself. For what each enacts for the other is a symbolic role, and the reality to which they may ultimately relate is no longer a place and a time, for all the anxious dating of that day in Dublin. It is an abstracted or more strictly an immanent pattern of man and woman, father and son; a family but not a family, out of touch and searching for each other through a myth and a history. The history is not in this city but in the loss of a city, the loss of relationships. The only knowable community is in the need, the desire, of the racing and separated forms of consciousness. Yet what must also be said, as we see this new structure, is that the most deeply known human community is language itself.[1]

We could move on from this ('the loss of a city' which is emblematic of a recognizable social structure where the characters can

---

[1] R. Williams, *The Country and the City*, London 1973, 245. Dr. Deane's lecture was delivered to the Cambridge Faculty of English on 12 Feb. 1974.

'find' themselves), to a consideration of the radically subversive quality of Joyce's language in his later writings—whose function is, among others, that of vanifying the literary *genre*, the novel, born in the eighteenth century precisely as the expression of the values of the new bourgeois society.

My purpose in the present paper is to try and pinpoint the moment and the place in Joyce's work when and where this process of rejection becomes absolutely clear—the rejection not only of the values that Stephen (*and* Bloom) uphold but also of those they fight against, since the characters are caught within the framework of a world which must be rejected *in toto*, and the aesthetic and ethical principles by which they seem to be guided are as tainted as the social and religious conventions which they condemn. I suggest that this process of rejection, the putting down of Stephen Dedalus, is fully realized in the central chapter of *Ulysses*, the tenth episode known as 'The Wandering Rocks'. I feel that the chapter was written for this purpose, so that it is worthwhile to see not only when and why it was conceived, but also how it reflects back on Joyce's previous work, from the *Epiphanies* to *A Portrait*, and how it fits into the overall structure of *Ulysses*.

The last question should perhaps be tackled first, because even in the extraordinary variety of modes of presentation that makes of each episode of the novel a nearly autonomous unit, 'The Wandering Rocks' looks anomalous, less integrated in the whole than the rest. It has been seen as a pause in the action; Stanley Sultan, in his most perceptive book on *The Argument of Ulysses* (1964), sees it as an interlude between the two halves of the book, the first preparatory and the second developmental.[1] None of the three main characters (or, in Williams's words, 'forms of consciousness') of the book is prominent in it: they appear only for brief moments, confused among the innumerable Dubliners (the full 'cast' of *Ulysses*) which people the nineteen sub-episodes (or rather eighteen plus a *codà*), constituting the chapter. Each sub-episode or section takes place in a different part of the town, like so many brief epiphanies, linked together by the transposition of

[1] Cf. C. Hart, *James Joyce's Ulysses*, Sydney 1968, 84.

short single sentences from each scene to the preceding or following ones, so as to underline the fact that all of them happen at the same time, though in different places, or very limited spaces. Time is still, only the spatial dimension is valid,[1] except in the first and last sections, describing the separate progresses of Father Conmee and of the vice-regal procession; the latter gives the sensation of time resuming its motion, as we realize how much ground has been covered by the different characters in their wanderings through Dublin streets since they were last seen in their respective sections—and, significantly enough, the royal cavalcade moves right into the next episode of *Ulysses*.

'The Wandering Rocks' is anomalous because of its static quality, an interlude or an epitome of the whole structure of *Ulysses* (its eighteen sections being a miniature reproduction of the eighteen episodes of the book), and at the same time a kind of essential *Dubliners*—each story of the earlier work being reduced to hardly more than an epiphanic moment. It harks back, in this way, to a poetics (rather than a 'technique') of prose writing— that of the 'epicleti' or 'epiphanies'—which by this time Joyce had discarded. Most of these short sections answer perfectly to the famous definition in *Stephen Hero*, when Stephen-Joyce, 'as he passed in his quest' along Eccles Street (which was to become the residence of the Blooms in the later novel), overhears an extremely banal conversation between a young couple standing in front of 'one of those brown brick houses which seem the very incarnation of Irish paralysis':

This triviality made him think of collecting many such moments together in a book of epiphanies. By an epiphany he meant a sudden spiritual manifestation, whether in the vulgarity of speech or of gesture or in a memorable phase of the mind itself.[2]

In a way, 'The Wandering Rocks' is just such a book of epiphanies—which the other episodes of *Ulysses* are emphatically not.

---

[1] See esp. R. Ellmann, *Ulysses on the Liffey*, rev. ed., New York, 1973, 97–101.
[2] J. Joyce, *Stephen Hero*, ed. T. Spencer, London 1944, 188.

Take for instance, from the fifth section, the conversation of Blazes Boylan in the fruit shop, after ordering a basket of fruit to be sent to Molly in Eccles Street:

> Blazes Boylan rattled merry money in his trousers' pocket.
> —What's the damage? he asked.
> The blond girl's slim fingers reckoned the fruits.
> Blazes Boylan looked into the cut of her blouse. A young pullet. He took a red carnation from the tall stemglass.
> —This for me? he asked gallantly.
> The blond girl glanced sideways at him, got up regardless, with his tie a bit crooked, blushing.
> —Yes, sir, she said.
> Bending archly she reckoned again fat pears and blushing peaches.
> Blazes Boylan looked in her blouse with more favour, the stalk of the red flower between his smiling teeth.[1]

Here is triviality, vulgarity of speech and gesture, in no way differing from the archetypal epiphany in *Stephen Hero*, the fragmentary conversation by the rusty area railing of the brown house in Eccles Street. Now why would Joyce suddenly start again collecting epiphanies so late in the day—in Bloomsday—only in this chapter of *Ulysses*, after having made Stephen himself poke fun at this kind of thing earlier in the book, in the 'Proteus' episode ('Remember your epiphanies on green oval leaves, deeply deep . . .')?

Moreover in 'The Wandering Rocks' these epiphanies are not even Stephen's—their inventor's—but the author's, since a distinguishing feature of the chapter is the absence of a hero, an individual consciousness in it: Stephen, Bloom and Molly are part and parcel of the epiphanies like the rest of the Dubliners appearing in the different sections. And this feature is stressed in a document which I find particularly relevant in connection with 'The Wandering Rocks'—the schema of *Ulysses* written by Joyce in Italian and sent in a letter to Carlo Linati on September 21st

[1] *Ulysses*, London 1937, 215.

1920, published by Richard Ellmann for the first time in his *Ulysses on the Liffey*.[1]

This schema has the advantage over the later ones—essentially the Gorman schema of late 1921,[2] which was streamlined into that included in Gilbert's book of 1930[3]—of having been compiled when the book was still being written (the last three episodes, the Nostos or Homecoming, were still to come, and indeed Joyce is rather vague about them in it), so that it does not read back in the text intentions and correspondences which were not there originally. It differs from the Gorman-Gilbert scheme mainly in respect of three headings which are either absent or substantially different in the latter:

1) *Simbolo*: while the Gorman-Gilbert scheme lists under this only one essential and at times arbitrary dominating image for each episode, the Linati schema provides a number of relevant symbolic correspondences. In the case of 'The Wandering Rocks' we find in Gorman-Gilbert only 'Citizens', while in Linati we have: 'Cristo e Cesare; Errori; Omonimi; Sincronismi; Rassomiglianze (Christ and Caesar; Errors; Homonyms; Synchronic correspondences; Resemblances)'.

2) *Senso (Significato)*, that is to say, *Meaning*, a heading not appearing in the later schemes and conceived rather like a traditional chapter heading, giving a key of the content of each episode; in the case of 'The Wandering Rocks' this seems extremely significant: *L'ambiente ostile*, i.e. the hostile environment, or rather, the hostility of the place—Dublin is a prison, to adapt Hamlet's phrase (this seems appropriate when we consider the frequent identification of Stephen with Hamlet).

[1] See Ellmann, *cit., passim*. I am quoting from a photocopy of the original ms. kindly provided by the Lockwood Memorial Library of the University of New York at Buffalo.

[2] A typed transcript from a schema circulated among Joyce's Paris friends in November 1921, preserved in the Croesmann Collection at Southern Illinois University; reproduced in *A James Joyce Miscellany, Second Series*, ed. M. Magalaner, Carbondale 1959, and in C. Hart, *op. cit.*

[3] S. Gilbert, *James Joyce's Ulysses: A Study*, New York 1930.

3) *Persone*, i.e. persons, characters: for each chapter, Joyce lists the 'actors' appearing in it, but not with the names they have in *Ulysses* but with those of their Homeric equivalents. In some cases (e.g. 'Hades') the list is quite long, but 'The Wandering Rocks' is the one exception. Instead of personal names, apart from Ulysses himself, we find here under this heading: *Oggetti, Luoghi, Forze*. Not people, but 'Objects, Places,' and—more relevant still, and we shall see later why—'Forces'; all things *outside* the characters, impinging on them, interfering with them.

This last feature of the schema singles out 'The Wandering Rocks' from the rest of the *Ulysses* episodes and gives it a particular significance. But before inquiring into it, it seems appropriate to recall another peculiarity of this episode which has been frequently remarked upon by previous critics: while to all the other chapters of the book there correspond specific episodes of the *Odyssey*, different adventures of Ulysses (or Telemachus), in this one case the Homeric reference is to an adventure that did *not* take place: Ulysses simply *heard* about the Wandering Rocks, the Symplegades that, clashing together, crush the ships that adventure between them. Circe told him that his homeward journey was fraught with dangers: either he sailed through the rock of Scylla and the whirlpool of Charybdis, or through the wandering, clashing rocks. Ulysses chose the first of the two routes, as did the Ulyssean heroes of Joyce's novel, who in episode 9 pass through Scylla and Charybdis. The fact that immediately after, in episode 10, unlike their Homeric prototypes, they attempt also the alternative route, corroborates the suggestion that the episode of 'The Wandering Rocks' came as an afterthought and was added by Joyce to the book as he was writing it, in the first place for the sake of structural symmetry (but by no means only for that reason).

Once again the Linati schema is revealing, as Ellmann rightly saw in his recent book. What is made clear by the early plan of *Ulysses*, while it is blurred in the later ones, is the rigorously ternary or triadic arrangement of the subject matter of the book together with its sharp division into two halves (emphatically marked by Joyce in a letter of 3 September 1920 to John Quinn, but ignored by most commentators, with the exception of Stanley Sultan and Clive Hart).[1] In the Linati schema Joyce marks a firm division, named after a part of the day, between each group of three episodes; they are worth listing briefly, since they disappeared in the later schemata.

The indication before the first chapter is ALBA (Dawn, with reference not to the actual hour of the day but to the emergence of the immature Stephen who, as indicated by the note replacing the usual references to the organs of the body for the first three chapters, 'is not yet suffering a body'). Before chapter 4, MATTINA (Morning); before chapter 7, MEZZOGIORNO (Noon). Then comes the main division of the whole book: between chapters 9 ('Scylla and Charybdis') and 10 ('The Wandering Rocks') Joyce wrote: 'GIORNO. Punto centrale—Ombelico' (Full day. Central point. Navel of the book). There is no reference to a part of the day between chapters 12 and 13, but this is an oversight since there occurs an obvious division, marked by a two-hour temporal gap: Bloom left the Cyclops' cave, Barney Kiernan's pub, at 6 p.m., in full daytime, and we find him in chapter 13 on Dublin rocks after dark—it is 8 in the evening—watching a firework (and Gerty MacDowell's) display; the word should have been SERA (evening). After the 'Circe' episode and before the last three chapters, the Homecoming of the hero, Joyce writes: 'MEZZANOTTE. Fusione di Bloom (Ul.) e Stephen (Tel.)' Midnight marks the moment of reunion and recognition of the two. Finally a note at the end of the schema stresses the circularity of the book—a remarkable anticipation of the basic structure of *Finnegans Wake*; it reads:

$$\text{NOTTE ALTA} - \text{ALBA}$$

Ulisse (Bloom)   Telemaco (Stephen)

The dead of night, personified by Ulysses-Bloom, through Penelope–Molly (*her* chapter, the last, bears the symbol of in-

[1] Cf. C. Hart, *cit.*, 84, and J. Joyce, *Letters*, I, ed. S. Gilbert, London 1957, 145.

finity, ∞, as its 'time'), leads to a new Dawn (Telemachus–Stephen), like that that marked the very beginning of the book.

True, the schema, though set down when the last part of the book was still unwritten, is an *a posteriori* device, a way of giving order, with nearly mathematical precision, to materials that had developed of their own accord. Without being a numerologist, Joyce took great pains to arrange his works in symmetrical patterns, even at the cost of being arbitrary. Take *Dubliners*: the stories were written casually enough, but he kept rearranging while adding to them, so as to create new symmetries. The original plan was to have ten of them, all on the same subject: paralysis.[1] Fifteen months later he arranged the *twelve* he had actually written or planned into four groups of three each (childhood, youth, maturity, public life);[2] when he found he had two more ready, he was careful to add them to the central groups, so as to have the sequence 3 + 4 + 4 + 3; and finally he added 'The Dead', a much longer story, outside the pattern, but with the same function of the additional movement, the *finale*, to a sonata or concerto, developing to the full the first theme of the first story: the books opens on the death of a paralysed priest, and closes on the theme of the identification of the living (in their state of paralysis) with the dead, under the white blanket of snow, the great leveller.

And the same care for balanced symbolic structures can be seen in the re-writing of the *Portrait*. *Stephen Hero* was a sprawling work, which had reached the twenty-sixth of its fifty or more chapters when Joyce stopped writing it; it became in the final version a neat five-part book, reflecting—as Francesco Gozzi shrewdly noticed[3]—the five books of the Pentateuch, from the Creation, i.e. Stephen's infancy, to the liberation of the Jews from the Egyptian bondage, or Stephen leaving the prison of Dublin for Paris; this is a bitterly ironic reversal of the Jews' homecoming, and the irony is squared by the fact (made quite

[1] See letter to C. P. Curran, July (?) 1904, *Letters, cit.*, I, 55.

[2] Letter to Stanislaus Joyce of about 24 Sept. 1905, *Letters*, II, ed. R. Ellmann, London 1966, III.

[3] F. Gozzi, 'Dante nell'inferno di Joyce', *English Miscellany*, 23, Roma 1972, 208–9.

clear in *Ulysses*) that Stephen's voluntary exile in Paris, where he is supposed to 'forge in the smithy of *his* soul the uncreated conscience of his race', is going to be an utter failure. The allusion to race on the last page of the final version of the *Portrait* suggests that Joyce had already thought of the Irish-Jewish equation, which he stated in full in the letter to Linati accompanying the *Ulysses* schema:

E' l'epopea di due razze (Israele-Irlanda) e nel medesimo tempo il ciclo del corpo umano ed anche la storiella d'una giornata (vita).[1]

But this is by the way. What I wish to underline is the tension between the first idea of *Ulysses* (the story of the Dublin Jew with an unfaithful wife, which Joyce planned in Rome in 1906 as an addition to *Dubliners*)[2] and the need he felt for a wider and wider frame for it, that would satisfy his sense of balance and structure. For a long time, in fact, Joyce did not know how many episodes there would be in *Ulysses*, but one thing was clear to him from the moment he decided to make the story into a long novel: that it was going to be, like Dante's *Divine Comedy*, a three-part book, reflecting, as the 'epic of the human body',[3] or rather (since he was aware of Fielding's model)[4] as 'the comic epic in prose of the human body', the trinitarian conception of the Body Divine, by substituting Molly, the flesh, for the Third Person, the Spirit or Holy Ghost. A *Human Comedy* but not a sprawling Balzacian *Comédie Humaine*: Dante and Homer were to preside over it. *Ulysses* should have three basic parts:

1. 'Telemachia', the adventures of Telemachus–Stephen Deda-lus, the Son in the parallel with the Holy Family and the

[1] 'Corrispondenza inedita di James Joyce e Carlo Linati', *Inventario*, III, 2, 1950, 98–99: 'It is the epic of two races (Israel–Ireland) and at the same time the cycle of the human body and also the little story of a day (life).'

[2] See letters of 30 Sept. and 13 Nov. 1906, *Letters, cit.*, II, 168, 190, 193.

[3] Joyce's own description to Frank Budgen, cf. F. Budgen, *James Joyce and the Making of Ulysses*, London 1934, rev. 1960, 21.

[4] See my 'Joyce and the Tradition of the Novel', *The Tightrope Walkers*, London 1956, 38–40.

Trinity. This corresponds also to Dante's *Inferno*: a defeated, immature, naïve idealist is back from his attempted escape to Paris, back not so much in the hell of Dublin as in his personal hell of frustration.

2. 'Odyssey' proper, the adventures of Ulysses-Bloom, the Father in the parallel with the Trinity, a putative father (most appropriately) in that with the Holy Family. This part is *Purgatorio*: Bloom has achieved maturity and, as a Wandering Jew, he is not the voluntary exile that Stephen wanted and failed to be, but the natural exile, a reasonable but ineffectual man, much nearer than Stephen to the ultimate goal, the acceptance of the human condition.

3. 'Nostos', or the Homecoming of Ulysses and his reunion with his (putative) son Telemachus, presided over by Molly-Penelope, i.e. Woman, the inverted symbol of motherhood in the Holy Family parallel and of the Spirit made Flesh in the Trinitarian. She *has* achieved the *Paradiso* of acceptance (yes) of the true human condition, which is the only way of overcoming that feeling of being hemmed in and interfered with that Stephen calls (episode 2) the nightmare of history. In her final subliminal monologue between sleeping and waking, Molly solves Stephen's nightmare, his fantasies (episode 3) and his and Bloom's hallucinations (episode 15), transforming them into ecstasy, a physical and sensual instead of a mystical ecstasy. She completes the human figure which is the secret structure of *Ulysses*—the epic of the Human Body—, being the final achievement of the continually frustrated quests of Stephen and Bloom.

Though the three-part division of the book was clear to Joyce from the start, he was confronted with the problem of subdivisions: how many chapters for each part? Dante's model, though a numerological feat (100 cantos divided in groups of 34, 33, 33, the first being a prologue) was too formidable. The *Odyssey* was awkward and unreliable, having been divided by later pedants into 24 cantos with a fine numerical progression, four for the 'Telemachia', eight for the 'Odyssey' proper, twelve

for the 'Nostos'; half of the poem was devoted to the least dramatic events, while the most interesting part, the wanderings of
Ulysses, was limited to eight cantos which used a synchronic
narrative technique anticipating Conrad's and Ford Madox
Ford's time-shifts and time-loops. Joyce, as it appears from his
letters, remained uncertain for a long time, so that as late as
November 1918, when he had already written nine episodes and
seven of them were in print in *The Little Review*, Ezra Pound
could still ask him:

> Has *Ulysses* 24 Odyssean books? I don't want to ask silly ques-
> tions, and I hope it continues forever, but people are continually
> asking ME about it.[1]

At that stage Joyce would have been hard put to it to reply. This
appears from his successive statements about the structure of the
book. The very first which has survived is in German, in a post-
card sent on June 16th, 1915—on the eve of his departure from
Trieste to Zurich—to his brother Stanislaus interned in Austria. It
reads:

> I have written something. The first episode of my new novel
> Ulysses is written. The first part, the Telemachia, consists of
> four episodes: the second of fifteen, that is to say, the Wander-
> ings of Ulysses: and the third, the Homecoming (*Heimkehr*) of
> Ulysses, of three more episodes.[2]

That gives us 4 + 15 + 3, for a total of twenty-two, a number
only two short of the *Odyssey*, but with a different distribution of
the parts, except for the Telemachia. But in 1915 he had merely
written a first draft of chapter one, and sketched out some of the
first and last episodes. He started working in earnest at *Ulysses* in
Zurich, after completing his play *Exiles*, and sent the first three

---

[1] *Letters, cit.*, II, 424.
[2] Photocopy of German original in S. Crise, *Epiphanies and Padographs,
Joyce a Trieste*, Milano 1967.

episodes (the *whole* of the Telemachia) to Pound towards the end of 1917. Only with prospect of publication he settled down to his task in 1918: by February he had completed episode 4, 'Calypso', by April episode 5, 'The Lotus Eaters', and on the 18th of May he could write to Harriet Shaw Weaver:

> If the Little Review continues to publish [*Ulysses*] regularly, [Huebsch] may publish as a cheap paperbound book the Telemachia, that is the first three episodes—under the title *Ulysses I*. I suggest this in case his idea be to keep the few persons who read what I write from forgetting that I still exist. The second part, the Odyssey, contains eleven episodes. The third part, Nostos, contains three episodes. In all seventeen episodes of which, including that which is now being typed and will be sent in a day or two, *Hades*, I have delivered six.[1]

But twenty days later, writing to his literary agent, Pinker,[2] about publishing separately the three parts, the number of the episodes has decreased from seventeen to sixteen: still three chapters for both first and last parts, but ten instead of eleven for the central one.

Writing steadily on, by November 1918 Joyce had completed the first nine episodes. He was determined to make capital out of all the adventures narrated in books v to xii of the *Odyssey*; the very mode of their telling, breaking down the chronological sequence, made them into models or archetypes of the different phases of the pilgrimage (the wanderings) of human life, so that they could easily be turned into emblems of nodal existential situations. But the significant Ulyssean episodes constituting the Odyssey proper added up to no more than eleven—an odd number which would hardly satisfy Joyce, confronted, in late 1918, with the problem of organizing the central part of his novel in such a way as to obtain, also *within* it, a play of symmetries and correspondences conforming to the basic ternary pattern of the whole; a play perhaps not so elaborate as the one recently worked

---

[1] *Letters, cit.*, I, 113.
[2] Letter of 9 June 1918, *Letters, cit.*, I. 114.

out with most ingenious thoroughness by Richard Ellmann in his *Ulysses on the Liffey*, but still complex enough. Joyce delighted in the discovery of unexpected and unplanned coincidences; all evidence points to the fact that he started unmethodically with some basic guiding principles in mind, and then elaborated and went over his work again and again as he discovered its endless analogical possibilities: he did not cast it in a mould in the first place, but moulded and remoulded *a posteriori* the rough cast he had made.

The Telemachia and the first three episodes of the Odyssey proper were easy to handle: to the adventures or wanderings of Telemachus–Stephen from 8 to 12 a.m. of June 16, 1904, there should correspond as many of Ulysses-Bloom in the same period of time. The two characters, like their Homeric originals, are following at the same time their separate routes in the world of Dublin: the two triads of chapters (1–3//4–6) mirror each other and the narrative techniques employed in both sets are the same: objective narration, dialogues and (interior) monologues, with variations in their respective proportions in each episode. Significantly, in the Linati schema under the heading *Tecnica* we find the same definitions for all six chapters: *Dialogo, Narrazione, Soliloquio* (with the single addition of *Preghiera* for Chapter 5); the more fanciful descriptions, such as *Catechism* for Chapter 2, *Narcissism* for 5 and *Incubism* for 6, are afterthoughts devised for the later schemata.

But the subsequent adventures, from noon onwards, don't allow this way of proceeding by parallel episodes: Bloom's day and Stephen's day must coincide and coalesce, each episode must involve both. In fact, at the level of 'technique' there is a break after Chapter 6: the alternation of dialogues and interior monologues within a narrative frame is no longer functional, when what matters is not the character of the hero, the 'adventurer', but the type of the adventure itself, which 'happens' and is valid as a symbolic experience undergone by Odysseus not as Odysseus but as the type of man, whether Bloom or Stephen or Everyman. From this moment on, the author must allow, as he explained to Linati, that ogni avventura (cioè ogni ora, ogni organo, ogni arte, connessi e immedesimati nello schema somatico del tutto) condizionasse anzi creasse la propria tecnica.[1]

So from this moment the techniques do vary: the seventh episode, 'Eolus', in the newspaper office, is ruled by the classical divisions of oratory and the rhetorical tropes; about the next, 'Lestrigonians' (Bloom is looking for somewhere to have lunch), Joyce told Frank Budgen:

In *Lestrigonians* the stomach dominates and the rhythm of the episode is that of the peristaltic movement,[2]

and indeed, *prosa peristaltica* is faithfully recorded as the technique of the chapter. In chapter 9, 'Scylla and Charybdis', the literary discussion in the National Library, where Stephen and the rest try to steer their course between dialectical antinomies (the Linati schema records as symbols: 'Hamlet/Shakespeare; Christ/Socrates; London and Stratford; Scholasticism and Mysticism; Plato and Aristotle; Youth and Maturity'), the technique is a series of dialectical whirlpools (*Gorghi* in the Linati schema).

Having reached this point, in Autumn 1918, Joyce realized that limiting the episodes of the central part of the book to the eleven Ulyssean adventures recorded by Homer would have seriously impaired the triadic progress of the work he had followed so far; *his* 'Odyssey proper' should include twelve chapters. Hence the decision, essentially for structural reasons of symmetry and formal balance, to introduce the new episode of 'The Wandering Rocks', the alternative adventure that had not actually happened to Ulysses. Why should the extra adventure be placed in the position it occupies now? The author knew that this was the mathematical centre of the book and wanted to take this opportunity for combining the basic ternary structure with a

[1] 'Corrispondenza inedita', *cit.*: 'each adventure (that is each hour, each organ, each art, connected and incorporated in the somatic schema of the whole) should condition or rather create its own technique' (the translations in *Inventario* and in *Letters*, I, 146–7, are misleading).

[2] F. Budgen, *cit.*, 21.

parallel binary structure: two halves of nine chapters each
(3 × 3). Episodes 9 and 10 should work as the hinges on which
the two halves would fold on each other, and so they must
coincide mirror-wise.

A misleading entry in the Gorman schema (omitted in Gilbert)
indicates the Symplegades (the Wandering Rocks) as equivalent
to 'Groups of Citizens'; in fact both Circe in Homer and the
Argonautica of Apollonius of Rhodes (which Joyce had recourse
to[1]) speak of only *two* clashing rocks—and it is significant that in
the Linati schema the citizens of Dublin or their Homeric counter-
parts are not listed, as we saw, among the *personæ* of the episode.
So the Symplegades are the exact counterpart of Scylla and
Charybdis, a booby trap for those who sail between them. As
Scylla and Charybdis represented the antimonies of intellectual
positions (Aristotle *v* Plato, Scholasticism *v* Mysticism etc.), so in
the newly-devised mirror episode 'the Wandering Rocks' must
represent another set of antimonies, no longer intellectual, but
concrete and rooted in history—actual *forces*, repressive and
oppressive; namely, the superstructures that crush the free manifestation of the human personality in a concrete social context—
the city—and in so doing paralyse its life.

The representation of a state of social and individual paralysis
was the main purpose of the stories in *Dubliners*, from the very
moment of their first inception.[2] *Stephen Hero* and, later, the
Portrait were meant to show the development of an individual
personality in this condition of surrounding paralysis, showing that
the only way out of it was voluntary exile. The exile theme had
been resumed by Joyce in 1915 in his play *Exiles* in order to take
it a step further: the voluntary exile did not consist (as Stephen and
young Joyce had believed at first) in leaving their homeland and
running away to Paris or Trieste—it was (Joyce had discovered
by now) an intellectual process taking place *inside* the personality
of the artist. This is the message carried over into *Ulysses*, where
Stephen is still the immature young man whose failure to achieve
a physical exile had resulted in frustration and ineffectuality.

[1] Cf. Ellmann, *cit.*, 91–92.
[2] See the already mentioned letter to C. P. Curran of July 1904.

'The Wandering Rocks' evokes precisely this situation, it is a backward look at the spiritual position which, in 1904, had prompted Joyce to write *Dubliners* and *Stephen Hero*. A well-known page of Frank Budgen, on the method followed by Joyce in writing this episode of *Ulysses*, is extremely instructive:

> To see Joyce at work on the *Wandering Rocks* [in the Winter 1918–19] was to see an engineer at work with compass and slide-rule, [...] Most of the characters of *Ulysses* appear in *Wandering Rocks*. Linking them together in unity are the paths of Christ and Caesar. Christ appears in the person of his servant, Father Conmee, and Caesar in the person of Caesar's servant, the Right Honourable William Humble, Earl of Dudley, Lord Lieutenant-General and General Governor of Ireland. These are the static forces of Church and State, restraining the destructive forces of wandering anarchic individualism.
>
> Christ and Caesar are here not in conflict—only in opposition. What is God's and what is Caesar's has been settled for them long ago. They are complementary and are so considered by the Dubliners who salute them and who are, in their turn, saluted or blessed by them.[1]

Indeed, Christ and Caesar are the first 'symbols' listed in the Linati schema for this episode. Budgen goes on:

> Joyce wrote the *Wandering Rocks* with a map of Dublin before him on which were traced in red ink the paths of the Earl of Dudley and of Father Conmee.[2]

By drawing on the map of Dublin those two routes, moving from West to East, one north and one south of the town centre on opposite sides of the Liffey, we have a visual representation of the very heart of Dublin caught between a pair of threatening pincers: Church and State, or, to use Stephen's definition in the first episode of *Ulysses*, 'two masters [...] the imperial British state and the holy Roman catholic and apostolic church'—which

[1] F. Budgen, *cit.*, 121.
[2] *Ibid.*, 122–3.

elicits Haines' lame apology: 'It seems history is to blame.'[1] And on *his* map Joyce did not mark the movements of the other Dubliners in the chapter.

The Linati schema makes the implications of this quite clear, not only by giving as the meaning of the episode 'the hostile environment', but by defining the technique used in it *Laberinto mobile fra due sponde* (in the later schemata it is merely 'Labyrinth'). The 'two banks' are obviously the two clashing rocks, benevolent Father Conmee on his way to visit an orphanage, and the Earl of Dudley going to open a bazaar in aid to Hospitals—a very benevolent undertaking.

Now we can see the reason for the introduction of the additional chapter (the adventure that never took place), and for its unusual form. It marks the moment of the final clarification and summarizes all Joyce's previous work. It is meant to fix once and for all an objective existential and historical condition; in other words, to exorcise Joyce's literary past, concentrating it in a series of epiphanies (an already discarded form of expression), and restating in this way, implicitly, that *Ulysses* is a new start, a creative rather than a destructive work, incorporating the old themes (paralysis and exile) only in order to explore new ground. The map of Dublin on Joyce's work-table is emblematic of the world from which his first two books, *Dubliners* and *A Portrait*, were born, and of their *raison d'être*. We are reminded of the oppressive superstructures, Church and State, only to be made aware of the fact that *Ulysses* shows how to dispense with them—that it is a gradual discovery of the one real structure, not a numerological conundrum for all its inner symmetries, but 'the somatic schema of the whole',[2] the figure of the human body; its 'epic' is complete and stands revealed only in the last episode, when Stephen (the young Joyce) and Bloom (the maturer wanderer) are reabsorbed in the liberating affirmation of acceptance of Molly Bloom. She represents the final integration of the human personality—three in one at this stage; but in *Finnegans Wake*, as

[1] *Ulysses, cit.,* 18.
[2] See the passage from the letter of 21 Sept. 1920 to Carlo Linati quoted in Italian above.

Stephen Heath has underlined,[1] the vital pulsation is from zero to one, from non-differentiation to identification. By the time Joyce had reached the tenth chapter of *Ulysses* the figure of Stephen had already withdrawn to its zero degree: though present, it had been effectually abolished as representative of the human condition. Which leads us back to Seamus Deane's remarks mentioned at the beginning, on the abolition of Stephen Dedalus and the purgation of society from the novel through an extremely punctilious epiphanic representation of it.

This, I believe, is the lesson of 'The Wandering Rocks'. The city is a labyrinth from which all escape is prevented by the dominant repressive forces. The way out of it is the process of identification, represented in *Ulysses* by Molly's 'yes'. The next step —a radical subversion operated in the first place on the linguistic level—is of course *Finnegans Wake*, a 'Meandertale':[2] from the pointless meandering within the nightmarish labyrinth of the two-dimensional world of history (the city and its loss, Raymond Williams reminds us, is history), to the tale, the story of the tortuous progress out of the nightmare, back to Neanderthal, to the origins of man through the rediscovery of language.

[1] In *Tel Quel*, n. 54, Été 1973. See also by Heath, 'Ambiviolences', *Tel Quel*, nn. 50 and 51.
[2] U. Eco, *Le forme del contenuto*, Milano 1971, 102–6; translated into French as 'Sémantique de la métaphore', *Tel Quel*, 55, Automne 1973, 25–46.

VI

The Novels of Joyce Cary

HELEN GARDNER

SOON after Joyce Cary's death in the spring of 1957 I gave a broadcast talk on him, though I felt and said that the moment after a writer's death was a bad time to speak of him, especially when, as Cary had done, he had been writing up to the very moment of his death. It is impossible to see the work in perspective, as a whole; it seems something broken off rather than finished. It has lost the life which contemporary writing has where we feel the excitement of 'work in progress' and in each new work look forward to what may be to come; but it has not reached the 'life beyond life' which works of past ages have. It is in a kind of 'No Man's Land'. I said then that I simply did not know how highly I should rate Joyce Cary's novels in twenty years, when they had come to live in my memory, or indeed whether they would live in my memory at all. Five years later, I was visiting Yale University and was asked to lecture. I chose Joyce Cary for my subject. The reason was that Dr James M. Osborn of Yale had given to the Bodleian Library a most notable benefaction: the Joyce Cary collection, comprising all his manuscripts, both of published and unpublished works, his letters, diaries, and his working library. I wished to pay tribute to this generous and imaginative gift, which has made it possible for those who want to study Joyce Cary's life and art to do so in depth, and to do so most appropriately in the city where he spent so much of his working life and had so many devoted friends.

One result of the Osborn benefaction has been a steady stream of young people working on the Cary manuscripts, usually with Mrs Davin to help them find their way in the bewildering mass of material. (As the person who edited and published his posthumous novel, *The Captive and the Free*, which he struggled to finish when paralysed and dying, she understands, as nobody else, his way of working.) Last summer, when one of these young people submitted a thesis on Joyce Cary for the D.Phil., and there was some discussion about the choice of an examiner, I volunteered. I had not re-read Cary's novels since I had lectured on them at Yale in 1962 and thought, with some trepidation, the time had come to do so. I spent a happy long-vacation, re-reading all the novels in chronological order in my spare time and found, to my delight, my feeling about them had not changed. They had not become 'period novels'; they were still for me rich and generous, original and moving. Though some were plainly more successful than others, none were without interest and, taken together, they added up to an impressively consistent body of work, solidly based on experience and observation, warmed by wide human sympathies and penetrated by an individual, imaginative conception of the nature of existence. I found to my pleasure that most of what I had said in 1957 on the radio and in my unpublished lecture at Yale in 1962 I could say again in 1974, and I was sorry that Joyce Cary's name had dropped out of discussions of the novel in this century.

In his own lifetime Joyce Cary's reputation was rather an odd one. He was on the whole ignored by academic critics, and not taken seriously by the most influential writers on the art of fiction. But he was not, on the other hand, a really popular novelist. His reputation was rather different in the United States, where he had an immense success with *The Horse's Mouth* (1944). When I was in California in 1954, on my first stay in the States, I found a great many more people who wanted to discuss his work with me than I had found in the universities in England. There also seemed to be more reference to him in literary journals on that side of the Atlantic. Since his death, although he has been the subject of some good books and the young people who work on him for their theses find him rewarding, his name has dropped out of literary discussion, and in some recent fairly full studies of the novel in the twentieth century he is hardly mentioned. On the other hand, his publisher thought him worth a Collected Edition (The Carfax Edition) in his lifetime, and the number of times some of the novels were reprinted, and their appearance in Penguins, showed he was widely read. I suspect he still is.

He was, I think, a genuinely original writer; but his originality was like that of his Gulley Jimson, the artist hero of *The Horse's Mouth*. It made him appear rather old-fashioned. 'I'm out of fashion,' says Gulley, 'before I was in fashion.' It had been suggested to him that he might sell better if he would paint some 'modern' pictures, and he tells us that Sara showed him 'a thing like a patchwork quilt, with a piece of a fiddle worked into it', as a model of what would be saleable. In the same way Cary's novels are not 'modern'. They are not written wholly in dialogue, or in some private allusive language, or back to front, or on the plan of some ancient myth, nor do they blend realism with fantasy or have any obvious symbolic reference. They are written as if some of the great masters of the twentieth-century novel had never written. Again, a good deal of comment on his novels as they appeared reminds me of Gulley's comment on the one critic who noticed his exhibition, who said that he was not an original artist at all but an imitator of two other artists: 'French artists, who were not only very old-fashioned, but quite different from each other.' He added: 'If they can't say you're bad, they say you aren't original.' So Joyce Cary was said to have gone back to the old picaresque tradition and to have taken Defoe as his model, and this absurdity was solemnly repeated in his obituary notices. In fact, Defoe's strength and the strength of the picaresque novel— and Defoe is, of course, not a picaresque novelist—is in narrative, which was Cary's most obvious weakness; and Cary's obsession with criminals and delinquents had a wholly different root from Defoe's. Defoe's was social: Cary's was religious. His central preoccupation was to find expressive form for his personal vision of human life. He was a man of exceptionally wide experience, of wide and undisciplined reading, and strong human sympathies. He was also gifted with great powers of observation—he is often startlingly shrewd in passing comment on human behaviour; but these gifts are at the service of his overmastering desire to render his sense of life. He wanted to create an image or symbol of what he called the 'character' of the world, and to express his intuition of the nature of reality as essentially 'free and personal', created for each one of us by the clash of 'universal consistencies' with 'individual character'.

The phrases are taken from the posthumously published Clark Lectures, *Art and Reality* (1958). No doubt, like the attempts of most artists to formulate the convictions that motivate their art, the lectures are vulnerable to professional philosophers. The importance of the attempt to formulate to Cary was very great. He did not publish a novel until he was over forty; after that they poured from him in a stream. His invention was liberated by some kind of period of crisis in which he worked out what he called his 'philosophy'. He had been writing long before that. His attics were full of drafts of novels and scenes from novels waiting to be worked out or left aside as unprofitable. He worked extremely hard at the novels he published, revising, re-writing, re-shaping, moving material about, discarding and adding. He would talk endlessly about technique and technical problems. The two sides of his nature were clearly seen in his fecundity of invention, his stress on the novelist's 'intuition' on the one side, and his labour at what he called 'joinery' or 'carpentering' on the other, the knocking into shape of the unformed matter of his books. He had, as it were, to make a whole length of cloth and out of that cut, shape, and piece together the garment. He had a vigorous artistic conscience and rejected admirable passages and highly wrought and vivid scenes if, as he revised, they came to seem inconsistent with the theme and form of the book as it grew to its final form. The most striking example is a long chapter discarded from *The Horse's Mouth* which his wife thought the best chapter in the book. This was privately printed by Herbert Davis on the press in the New Bodleian for distribution to his friends the Christmas before his death, under the title *The Old Strife at Plant's*. Behind the books as published there lay a mass of imagined stories, actions, scenes and characters and in some cases whole drafts. He knew much more about the people in his novels than he put into them as published. This accounts partly for the sense of fullness, of a wealth of material, that the novels give. They are all crowded.

This richness was the fruit of a very rich and varied experience of life, and an openness to the experience it provided.

He was born of an old Anglo-Irish family which had settled in Northern Ireland under Elizabeth I, and he spent his childhood in the wild and beautiful coastal county of Donegal on the Inishowen peninsula, near the mouth of Loch Foyle. He kept all his life the look of a man who had ridden and fished and sailed a boat since childhood. An intensity of happiness that is almost ecstatic runs through the beautiful book he made out of his Irish boyhood, *A House of Children.* In all his books the sense of pure physical pleasure is very strong: the feeling of the joy of being alive and using one's body to the limit. His favourite among novelists was Tolstoy, and in this at least he resembled his master: I am thinking of scenes like that of Levin harvesting in *Anna Karenina.* But he suffered also in childhood the loss of his mother; and this strengthened independence of spirit in him and made him rate courage and faith, which is the root of courage, as the fundamental human virtues. He was educated at Clifton College and Trinity College, Oxford and also studied art at Edinburgh and in Paris. He went on painting all his life. His house was full of portraits of his wife and children and he drew a remarkable self-portrait just before his death. (*The Old Strife at Plant's* was illustrated by him, the sketches coloured according to his instructions by the Davis and Davin children.) From Paris he went to fight as a volunteer in the Balkan Wars, returned to Ireland for a short spell of administrative work, and then joined the Nigerian Political Service, fought in the Nigerian regiment in the 1914–18 war, and after the war was sent to be magistrate executive officer in a remote up-country district, Borgu, in northern Nigeria. Professor Molly Mahood, formerly Professor of English at Ibadan, has written finely of Joyce Cary and Africa. He sank wells, 'from which the women of Kaiama, swathed in bright cottons, still draw clean water. He built zongas, safe inns for traders. He built trestle bridges. He constructed Borgu's first motorable road—still today, when one drives over it at 60 miles an hour, one of the best stretches in the division.'

He had to give up a career in Africa on account of ill-health, and in middle life he settled in Oxford to make himself into a writer. Intertwined with what looks like a life of restless adventuring was a personal life of deep, simple and stable satisfactions. He was supremely fortunate in his marriage and had great happiness as father of four sons and, at the end of his life, as a grandfather. He also had a genius for friendship and once he had given affection gave it for ever. The stability of family relationships, the force of affection, and the sense of responsibility that affection arouses and feeds on, so that we look after those we love and love those we look after, is one of the recurrent themes in his novels. Many people who met this handsome, exquisitely groomed North Oxford gentleman, this devoted husband and father, with his charming slightly old-fashioned courtesy of manner, and his obvious delight in the traditional and beautiful decencies of civilized life, found it difficult to understand how he could be the writer of the novels: the sympathetic creator of the delinquent Charlie, the dishonest Sara Munday, the ranting, roaring Gulley Jimson, and all the other law-breakers, religious fanatics, eccentrics, peculators and adulteresses who occupy the foreground of the novels. They overlooked what is the peculiar strength of the novels. They give us, along with these rebellious forgers of their own world, other figures presented with equal sympathy, the sober, the responsible, the loyal, the sons of Martha: Rudbeck the magistrate as well as the romantic clerk, Mr Johnson, the soldier Bill and his wife Amy as well as Bill's sister Lucy, who goes off with the Benjamites, and Bill's brother, the old lawyer, Thomas, who beautifully blends an innate conservatism with attempts to break out into freedom. Professor Mahood has rightly said that it was in Africa, ruling a province that Joyce Cary discovered one of his main themes: the twin calls of loyalty to family, to tribe, to country, to profession, and of creative freedom, individual fulfilment.

The African novels are remarkable for their author's first-hand knowledge of the day-to-day realities of colonial administration and for their author's imaginative sympathy with rulers as well as ruled. Their obvious subject is the clash of cultures, the drama of a primitive people being forcibly educated and dragged at breakneck speed into the twentieth century, confronted with western techniques and with western cultural patterns. They display the continuing strength of the old tribal culture resisting disintegration, and the dilemma of the African hovering between two worlds, each with its claim on his imagination and with its own moral imperatives. This is not an original subject. What gives these books, *Aissa Saved, The African Witch, Mr. Johnson* (the finest of them), their special quality is the author's involvement and the width of his sympathy. They are the novels of a man who has himself been a responsible actor in the scenes he paints. In this they are strikingly different from E. M. Forster's *A Passage to India,* a novel by a sensitive observer of a scene, a visitor, which divides the human race into native sheep and administrative goats. But Cary's African novels are much more than political novels, giving a picture of the day-to-day realities of colonial administration. Africa presented him in an acute form with the paradox that human beings can work together and love each other very deeply and in a measure understand each other, but that they inhabit different worlds; for to each one of us the world is continually created by our imaginations feeding on and creating our experience. The clash of African and European imaginations is subsumed into this larger theme of the clash of all human imaginations. What to other writers has been a source of dismay, the separateness of human experience, that each man is an island, was to Cary a proof of the essential unity of mankind. Child and adult, black and white, old and young—all were seen by him as living by their dream, their vision of themselves, creating themselves and their world by the exercise of their most essential human attribute, their freedom. Rudbeck's vision drives him to build the road, as Cary had himself built a great road, and to do this he breaks rules and overlooks Treasury regulations and turns a blind eye on the methods by which his clerk and helper, Mr Johnson, recruits and pays labour. Mr Johnson, the poor government clerk, has a vision of himself as a splendid government servant of the King of England, friend and helper of Rudbeck. This leads him to run into debt, steal and pilfer, give glorious parties to celebrate imaginary triumphs, and in the end kill the store-keeper whose till he has robbed. At the close they are brought together: the magistrate who must carry out the sentence and the murderer who must be hanged. Without Johnson the road could not have been built; and to the end he regards Rudbeck as his friend and wants to save him trouble. They are bound by a shared enterprise. The last pages of *Mr. Johnson* are among the most moving Cary ever wrote. Rudbeck appeals for a reprieve on the grounds of the prisoner's youth and instability. It is refused. He goes through all the horrible preparations for a judicial hanging—but he cannot let it end like that. He goes in and shoots the boy himself as Johnson had asked him to do: 'I like you to do him yourself, sah! You my friend.' The last words of the book are Rudbeck's: 'I couldn't let anyone else do it, could I?'

As well as the African books, Joyce Cary wrote two remarkable novels about children. *A House of Children* is his most exquisite book, and again is concerned with the clash of two worlds; the world of childhood, and the world of adult life. The children are on the verge of the grown-up world and the older of them, to the bewilderment of the younger, are growing out of the world of direct experience which is childhood, into the conceptual and ordered world of the grown-ups, which seems mysterious and absurd to the children absorbed in their own world of immediate joys and sorrows. The other, *Charley is my Darling*, is a brilliant study of a childish delinquent, the town-evacuee Charley sent to the West Country at the outbreak of war from a London slum. He is found to be lice-ridden and has to have his head shaved and this makes him a butt of the others. But being 'a child of imagination and nerve' he fights back, makes himself leader of a gang, and embarks on a series of housebreaking enterprises which become more and more daring, fruitless and destructive, to satisfy his imagination of himself as a great desperado. When Cary was asked how he knew so much about young offenders, he said it was because he had a good memory of his own childhood; but added that he was a lucky child whose elders gave him a clear sense of right and wrong, and encouraged him to exercise his imagination, so that he was neither bored nor confused. Charley, like Mr Johnson, is the victim of an imagination that has outrun the discipline of facts, and is operating in a moral void. The nearest he comes to adult life is in his relation with another outcast, the devoted deaf child Liz and this, since he gets her with child, is, ironically, the most serious count against him when the law catches up with him and he comes before the courts.

Both *Mr. Johnson* and *Charley is my Darling* are third person novels written in the present tense. Cary defended his use of the present tense, which reviewers had complained of, on the grounds that he was trying to present direct experience, not history; that the subject of *Mr. Johnson* was Johnson's confused apprehension of the world, his attempts to come to terms with the flux of experience; and that the use of the past tense would destroy this. The desire to present experience directly and not by description, and his conception of each human imagination creating its own world made him turn to the use of the first person. But he could not be content with the solipsism inherent in the first-person novel, and this drove him to his most ambitious work—his two trilogies. The first of these, which began in 1941 with *Herself Surprised* and went on with *To be a Pilgrim* and *The Horse's Mouth*, is, I think, the work by which he will finally be judged. The second trilogy is too laboured and too ambitious in its scope, and too weighed down by theories and information. It is not based on direct experience but on what Cary rather grandiosely called his 'research'. The world of high politics was not a world of which he had real knowledge, and the adult Chester Nimmo is not credible. But this criticism does not apply to the second book of the trilogy, *Except the Lord*. Here Cary's understanding of childhood, his sympathy for nonconformity in religion and in politics, and for the harshness of the life of the poor in late Victorian England give the book an authenticity which the first and last novels of the trilogy lack. It is one of the finest treatments in fiction of what so puzzles continental observers of the English political scene: the strength of the ties in England between religious and political radicalism.

The first trilogy was designed, as he said himself in the preface to the Carfax edition of the novels, 'to show three characters, not only in themselves, but as seen by others. The object was to get a three dimensional depth and force of character. One character was to speak in each book and describe the other two as seen by that person.' The centre of his plan, as he said, was 'character': the characters of his three leading persons in conflict with each other and with other characters, and with the 'character' of their times and beyond that with final 'character', by which he said he meant 'the shape of things and feelings which are "given"'. In other words the books were to be about 'life' in three senses: the life of individuals, the life of the times they lived through, and life generally, in the sense that we say 'Life is or is not like that' or 'Oh well, that's life.' It may be said that every good novel is about life in these three senses and there was no need for Cary to attempt anything so complicated as his trilogy to convey them. He said himself that the scheme did not fully come off. This is partly but not wholly true. Some partial failures are more success-ful than some successes.

The first book is Sara's. It is her own story told by herself. She is in prison, convicted of what appears to be the mean crime of having robbed her doting old employer, Thomas Wilcher, who was on the verge of marrying her when his relations stepped in, got the police to search her luggage, and removed him from her clutches. She has been much shocked and startled by the judge's comment at her trial, that she had behaved 'like a woman without any moral sense'. She tells her story so that 'some who read this book may take warning and ask themselves before it is too late what they really are and why they behave as they do'. In fact, far from having been brought to a sense of her guilt, Sara, in her long monologue, reveals a conscience fundamentally at peace with itself.

'What people really are and why they behave as they do' is Joyce Cary's main subject, but if he is described as a novelist of the conscience, he is so in a peculiar sense. Unlike almost all novelists who concern themselves with the springs of human actions, Joyce Cary is not interested in the conscience that says 'No'. His con-cern is with the conscience that says 'Yes'. The moral imperatives which govern a human life are what interest him, the main-springs of conduct. His characters are all people who live by an individual faith and follow the promptings of their own spirits.

They are all untroubled by guilt. Most of the novelists who have explored the conscience in this century have been Catholics. Joyce Cary stands out as the novelist of the Protestant conscience.

Normally the novelist interested in the conscience and moral problems chooses to show a *crise de conscience* and shapes his plot dramatically to lead to some moment of crisis in which essential moral character is revealed by choice, or punished or rewarded for choice. Joyce Cary's concern was not with crisis but with the whole flow of a life, with what gives a human life continuity and consistency. This led to his main difficulty as a novelist. His books are crowded with characters, lively scenes and comic or pathetic incidents; but there is a curious sense that all the time, although we are moving forward, we are standing still. He had so strong a sense of what persists in a human personality, of seeing the same eyes looking out of the face of an old woman as looked out of the face of a child, that the passage of time and the course of events seem detached from and almost irrelevant to the person living through them. This gives the novels an episodic effect. None of his characters can be said to develop or change with experience, so that the episodes become illustrative of what they are, rather than significant elements in a design. The important thing about Sara Munday is not that she ends her story in prison, but that she is what she is. But what is she?

Well, to herself she is someone for whom life has been too complicated, victim of her own kind heart and what she calls her 'nature', and of bad luck. But to Thomas Wilcher, her old master, who speaks in the second book, *To be a Pilgrim*, she is something quite different. The old lawyer, fussy, timid, disreputable, the feeble member of a strong family, with his sordid little meannesses and his furtive little lusts, sees the woman his family have rescued him from as the person who 'saved his soul alive'. Virtually a prisoner in his old home, he declares his 'truth about Sara'.

> They see Sara as a fat red-faced cook of forty-six. And they believe that this cook, a cunning and insinuating country woman, who had deceived two men before, swindled me and

robbed me, and so enslaved me, by her sensual arts and smooth tongue, that I promised to marry her ... The truth is, that when Sara came to me, I was a lost soul. I had become so overborne by petty worries, small anxieties, that I was like a man lost in a cave of bats. I wandered in despair among senseless noises and foulness, not knowing where I was or how I had got there. I loathed myself and all my actions; life itself. My faith was as dead as my heart; what is faith but the belief that in life there is something worth doing, and the feeling of it.

But it is not because Sara became his mistress that she renewed the springs of faith in him. It was because she looked so well after his house.

I remember still how, within a week of my coming to Tolbrook, she showed me a table in the saloon, which had been scratched by some careless maid with a gritty duster.

'It ought to be seen to, sir. It's such a lovely polish,' and she passed her hand over its surface in a caress.

'Yes, yes, Mrs. Jimson,' I said, 'that's a very fine table—a very remarkable table. It's been in this room more than a century, since it was made for this very room', and I saw again, I rejoiced in the beauty and distinction of the old table. Sara had renewed to me that joy which is the life of faith. And so in those days, while she cleaned the house and set it to rights, after many years of lazy and careless maids, I came to feel its value, to enjoy its grace.

No doubt any connoisseur, any collector, some bored old millionaire when he shows off his treasures, is seeking in your praise, the resurrection and the life. But he could not get the kind of appreciation which Sara gave, out of her generous and lavish heart, to my old things at Tolbrook and Craven Gardens. She delighted in caring for them, as if they had been her own.

We say of such a one as Sara, 'a good servant', and think no more of it. But how strange and mysterious is that power, in one owning nothing of her own, to cherish the things belonging to another.

But to Gulley Jimson, the painter, who speaks in the third novel, *The Horse's Mouth*, Sara is not a 'lavish and generous heart' and her desire to cherish and put things to rights is not a virtue. It is part of her self-love and her desire to manage. He goes to call on her when she is an old woman and he an old, still unsuccessful painter, like her just out of prison.

But when we came to Sara's door it was new painted, and the door knob shining like rolled gold. Sara all over, I thought, you can see she's adopted that door-knob—loves it like herself. Rub the little darling up and give it a chance to look its best. Sara for cleaning and washing. Loved slapping things about. Getting off her steam. See Sara in her bath washing herself. Like a cat. Almost hear her purr. I didn't know whether to draw her or to bite her. And I did give her one with the back brush which made her jump. Oh Gulley what was that for? Just to let you know there's somebody else in the world. Good sketch I did of her—with the same back brush. Right arm in the air. Elbow cutting up against the window. Hair over left shoulder catching the light. Lime green outside. Head bent over to the left—line of the cheek against the hair. Lips pushed out. Eyes dropped. Looking at her breasts. Serious expression. Worship.
      And all the same she was a fine woman. She made me mad every way. Regular born man-eater. . . .

But what *is* Sara in reality? And what *is* Thomas Wilcher? Is he the master of Sara's imagination to be cherished and made happy, who cannot help his little ways, or the pilgrim soul voyaging forward by the light of a renewed faith of his own imagination, or is he the man Gulley saw: 'A little grasshopper of a man. Five feet of shiny broadcloth and three inches of collar. Always on the jump. Inside or out. In his fifties. The hopping fifties. And fierce as a mad mouse.'
      And what is Gulley Jimson? Is he a helpless person who needs a woman to look after him and manage his life, or is he an in-spired artist, an original genius, or is he a fraud, a selfish sponger and brutal egoist and moreover an old self-intoxicated bore? For this is one of the penalties of Joyce Cary's method. We have to listen so long to a single voice; and if, as with Gulley, it is a voice that shouts, we become tired and long for another voice

and other worlds, to be in the company of someone who is not in a state of permanent excitement, and in a world in which everything is not distorted by an over-vivid imagination. Another penalty is that as the person goes on communicating his own vision of himself he tends to become more and more a humour character, someone displaying his well-known oddities. He becomes as he talks less real and more like Mr. Micawber: a 'character part' rather than a character.

To show characters from different sides, to let them express themselves, to vary the point of view from which someone is seen is nothing new in the novel. If this were all that Joyce Cary had wanted to do he had no need to invent this extremely difficult and cumbrous form which set him such very difficult artistic problems. In the last book, for instance, of his second trilogy, *Not Honour More*, he found himself committed to a narrator who could only express himself in clichés, in a style modelled on the style of army instructions, and with a vocabulary like that of a police officer giving evidence. It was necessary for his whole conception that Jim, the unreflective and inarticulate, should be the last speaker, and he showed considerable skill in modifying Jim's way of speaking enough to make the book just readable without destroying his characteristic lack of expressiveness. All the same, it was an almost impossible task he set himself, as if Jane Austen had decided she must re-tell the story of *Emma* through the mouth of Miss Bates, or Dickens had let Mrs Nickleby tell the story of *Nicholas Nickleby*.

What drove him on was not wilful eccentricity, or sheer delight in setting himself difficult technical problems to solve, though he loved a technical problem, but his individual vision of human life. What the trilogy form expresses is the absence of that 'point of view' which, since Henry James discussed it, is what we all look for in a novel. Henry James could call the story of Isabel Archer *The Portrait of a Lady*. But *Herself Surprised* cannot be called *Portrait of a Woman*. It is not even a self-portrait, because Sara owns she does not understand herself. At the end she only knows that she can and must go on: 'A good cook will always find work, even without a character, and can get a new character in twelve months, and better herself, which, God helping me, I shall do, and keep a more watchful eye, next time, on my flesh, now I know it better.' And if we take the three books together and say that they make up a portrait of a woman, it is like one of those modern portraits in which profile and full face have become mixed up, and in which the sitter is less clearly recognizable than in a portrait painted from a single viewpoint. Cary himself owned in his preface to *Herself Surprised* that his scheme for the three novels had not come off: that the three books only gave 'aspects of Sara', true 'in their own context', and that a lot of Sara was not there, had had to be cut out. 'There wasn't room for her,' he said ruefully.

His novels sprang from his sense of the mystery of human personality and the mystery of what makes experience significant and meaningful to individuals. The central 'invisible sun within us', by which we live, fascinated him. He could not claim to know the final truth about the creatures of his imagination if they were to be true symbols of the human beings he saw in the world around him. He could only go on telling us more and more about them. With this refusal to select a view-point from which the final truth about a person can be seen there went as a corollary a refusal to judge. The stories he tells continually demand and excite moral judgments in the reader, and the characters continually express moral views and criticize themselves and others. The novels are full of moral feeling. But the design of his novels does not impress on us, as the design of most great novels does, an implicit moral judgment on the actions of the characters and the whole course of the story. His novels are rather designed to express a religious apprehension of human beings as objects of delighted contemplation. Although he appears superficially a realistic novelist, and a creator of humorous and eccentric characters, he really has far more in common with a poet such as Wordsworth than with Defoe or Fielding. Sara restoring old Wilcher's faith and courage by the love she showed for his furniture is a purely Wordsworthian subject. Like all natural contemplatives he chooses for his contemplation what excites his admiration and love, what he finds wonderful in human nature. Unlike the modern school

of theological novelists he 'chooses not the dark side for contemplation'. It is the virtues of men and women that interest him.
Just as in Wordsworth's imagination ordinary men and women
are transformed into mysterious and august figures, so that his
world is peopled with Solitaries, so the people of Joyce Cary's
world for all their immense variety in type and class, and personal
history, and manner of expression, are essentially akin. His
imagination presents a world of Creators and Preservers. His
world is peopled by images of the Divine creative and preserving
energy which keeps the world in being, the energy which Blake
said was 'eternal delight'.

His characters are the creations of a vision, and again and again
in his novels he gives us scenes which have a visionary quality,
expressing his sense of the 'character' of life itself as a complex of
personal values. There is one towards the end of To Be a Pilgrim.
Old Wilcher, when rescued from Sara, was taken charge of by
his niece Ann, a young woman doctor, in his old and beautiful
family house which he had cherished all his life. His nephew
Robert arrives, the two young people marry, and Robert takes
over farming the estate. There is no barn for his fine, new threshing
machine, so he breaks into the beautiful Adam drawing-room,
which is just the height to take his machine, and establishes it
there. The conception is wholly unrealistic and the scene as old
Wilcher looks at it becomes an image of the universe: of 'central
peace subsisting at the heart of endless agitation', and of 'past and
future gathered'; it also is an image of England at war. The novel
was published in 1942.

> The huge machine, like a species of Roman siege engine, towers
> in the middle of the floor, driven by a tractor among the
> broken laurels. The driving band passes through one of the
> beautiful windows from which the panes have been knocked out
> of the sashes. The carts are backed in turn along the west side,
> brushing the painted walls. And behind Farley, who is feeding
> to Robert on top of the machine, I see over the middle window
> a rural trophy in plaster of delicate scythes and sickles, sheaves
> and hayforks, tied up in pale blue ribbon. But the thick chaff
> dust, which lies along every panel moulding like yellow snow,

is already hiding their beautiful detail, characteristic of Adams' refinement.

Farley's head, when he takes his stand upon a new load, almost brushes the cupids on the ceiling, painted among Adams' fine plaster by Angelica Kaufmann. They seem to be flying round the old man's bald brown skull like cherubim round one of El Greco's saints. He feeds with deliberation, throwing each sheaf where it is wanted, and the expression on his dried-up face, wrinkled as an old fence post, is that of an eternal patience.

The girl Molly lifts off the filled sacks and twisting up their loose necks drags them across the floor with her huge arm to the side door, where Robert, by taking out a panel and knocking down the bricks, has made a loading platform. The grinning and horned Pan, who, in white marble, plays upon his syrinx, under one end of the magnificent mantelshelf, famous among the scholars of architecture, carries on one horn some labourer's luncheon, tied up in a red handkerchief; and round his waist, mixed with the marble flowers and grasses, hangs a bunch of real onions on a string. His grin reminds me of Robert's smile.

The whole building, floor, walls and roof, shakes and thunders, and through the mist of fine dust rising and falling in the air on every draught, long bars of yellow sunlight decline, hiding the far end of the room in a blue shadow.

Ann has placed herself on a pile of sacks, between two windows. She has a book open on her lap but does not read. She knits and looks occasionally out of the window, or at Jan running about among the mountains of chaff which rise below the thresher, or at Robert high up on the machine; but always with her pre-occupied air, like someone who looks at a passing landscape, a strange child, a figure on some distant mountain.

In a pause of the roar, while the tractor is stopped to tighten the driving band, she says, 'That child is full of fleas from the draff'. And Robert's voice answers from among the gods and goddesses on the ceiling, 'He may as well get used to 'em now'.

The two old men, who are shovelling this draff away to keep it from swallowing up the machine, look at the child with mild speculative faces. They are those old labourers, twisted and knotted almost out of human shape, lame, stooped, with distorted arms and crooked, swollen fingers, who are seen only in harvest time, when they creep out again into the sun, to do some humble task which does not need much strength . . .

I sit in the armchair, a tattered bergère, in white and gilt, last of the drawing-room furniture; and the very ruin of this beautiful room is become a part of my happiness.

Happiness is a very rare subject in the modern novel. It is, to me, the greatest of Joyce Cary's gifts that he can communicate his sense of the 'character' of life as capable of perpetually flowering into happiness and joy. He is a comic novelist without a trace of the satirist in his composition, and his subject is a universe freely bringing forth delight.

VII

The Pursuit of Influence

WOLFGANG CLEMEN

RESEARCH into literary influences has steadily diminished in importance over the last few decades. Doubt has been cast on the very validity of an analysis of literary influence as a contribution towards the understanding of a work of literature. The more we chose to concentrate on the text itself, not taking into consideration any criteria outside this frame of reference, the more sceptical the attitude towards studies dealing with sources and influences was bound to become. We have been told to see and evaluate the work of art as something unique and autonomous and not as something derivative, which can be traced back to sources, traditions, and influences. In analysing literary influences the connection between cause and effect appears particularly uncertain. Influences, as well as sources, undergo a considerable change in the process of re-creation; in the finished work they may emerge as something new and quite different, bearing only an outward and often superficial resemblance to their point of departure. The final work transcends its sources and materials and also the influences which went into creating it. Moreover, an influence tends to detach itself from its origin. Not what a work of literature actually is, but what the 'influenced poet' believes it to be, determines the nature of the influence. The positivist belief in detecting an influence by pointing out similarities, parallels and textual resemblances has given way to a more pessimistic attitude as to the possibility of diagnosing influences with any degree of certainty.[1] Besides, similarities which had been attributed to influence could in a number of cases just as well be explained by

---

[1] What J. B. Leishman wrote about the influence of Donne may be symptomatic: 'Where fashion and mode are active the detection and disintrication of "influences" become formidably difficult.' (*The Monarch of Wit*, 1962, Ch. I).

analogy, by the fact that similar conditions may lead to comparable results for several authors writing at the same time. And even if by means of textual parallels an influence could be demonstrated beyond doubt, it would remain superficial and should be considered of secondary importance. Some critics even denied that the influence of a poet can ever extend below the surface. 'What he can and does transmit is the accidents, the idiosyncrasies, the mannerisms of genius. . . . But what he cannot give or they receive is the quality that makes him what he is. That is incommunicable,' wrote J. L. Lowes as early as 1919.[1] The notion that we could explain a work of literature by identifying its sources and influences has been discredited and most critics to-day would agree with what T. S. Eliot wrote about the creation of a poem: 'that something comes into being which is new—in the sense that it cannot be explained by literary or other influences'.[2]

But apart from these doubts which concern the methods of influence-studies, the concept of literary influence itself remains uncertain. What is the proper domain of literary influence? Would it, for instance, also include conscious borrowing from another author, imitation, pastiche and plagiarism, the use of inherited conventions and literary traditions, the adoption of verse-forms, methods of composition and other such elements which in literary history are invariably handed down from one poet to another? And how is influence related to literary reputation, 'reception', and contemporary taste? In our histories of literature the label 'influence' is used for a great many different things, which vary as widely as the types and kinds of literary works to which they are applied. In examining the complex phenomenon 'literary influence' we would therefore have to differentiate in many ways, delimiting the sphere of influence and clarifying several preliminary questions as to the underlying principles and the *raison d'être* of 'influence'. But in doing so we would come across new doubts affecting not only the results, but also the aims and the methods of influence studies. It is worth remembering that Virginia Woolf in *To the Lighthouse*

[1] J. L. Lowes, *Convention and Revolt in Poetry*, 1919.
[2] Preface to L. Vivante, *English Poetry*, 1950.

96   ESSAYS AND STUDIES 1975

characterized Charles Tansley by repeatedly describing him as working on a book about 'the influence of something on somebody'.

However, despite all these reservations and the objections which have been raised against the usual trend of influence studies[1], we cannot deny that influence is not only a frequent but in some cases also a significant phenomenon in the history of literature. For as soon as we look not only at a single work but rather at a whole group of related poems, novels or plays, as soon as we try to come to grips with periods, developments, genres, schools of poetry, we become aware that influences play an important role as links within a network of interrelated works. This is particularly true if we view literature, to use T. S. Eliot's phrase, 'not as a collection of the writings of individuals but as organic wholes, as systems in relation to which, and only in relation to which, individual works of literary art have their significance'.[2]

If we want to gain insight into the 'constant give and take' (T. S. Eliot) which constitutes literary history, we shall find that influence is one of the keys to a better understanding of these interrelationships. Yet its function in revealing these relationships and interdependences must not be overemphasized; it is merely ancillary. Here again a common misunderstanding has evolved which resulted in an all too positivist evaluation of what was visible on the surface. Influences can only point to existing relationships, being symptoms rather than causes. The statement that an innovation or a major change in the development of literary genres has been brought about or even 'caused' by foreign influences or by the influence of an earlier poet on a later one must be qualified. For the change which critics attributed to this influence must have taken place beforehand. An altered conscious-

---

[1] See Ihab H. Hassan, 'The problem of influence in Literary History: Notes towards a Definition', *Journal of Aesthetics and Art Criticism*, XIV (1955); Haskell M. Block 'The Concept of Influence in Comparative Literature', *Yearbook of Comparative and General Literature VII* (1958); Claudio Guillén 'The Aesthetics of Influence', *Comparative Literature* vol. I, Proc. of the Second Congress of the ICLA (1959); Anna Balakian, 'Influence and Literary Fortune', *Yearbook of Comparative and General Literature* II (1962).

[2] 'The Function of Criticism', *Selected Essays*, 1934, p. 23.

ness, a changed attitude, or at least a readiness and a disposition towards change must have been there for influences to work. Influences are outward signs of more deep-seated processes of change and integration. They are, as it were, the waves visible on the surface which denote underlying currents. They therefore demand interpretation which goes beyond the detection of textual or structural similarities. For any major and significant literary influence which may be established provokes questions such as 'Why could this influence produce its effect at this precise moment, with this particular poet?'; 'What were the conditions which made possible the reception and assimilation of this influence?'; 'Which tendency in the poet himself was made articulate by his choice of a new model, by his becoming "subject to the influence of x" (the usual phrase for describing this process in our literary histories)?' 'What was the larger context, the wider literary network to which this influence contributed; and which it helps us to decipher?'

Research on specific influences has rarely been conducted with questions such as these in mind, although as a principle of criticism, as a methodological requirement, these problems have been touched upon by our leading critics.[1] There are many studies on the influence of single authors but no comprehensive and systematic study of the whole phenomenon has as yet been attempted which would discriminate between the various types of influence, comparing the functions and forms of literary influence in relation to periods and authors, and inquiring into the conditions and motivations which underlie the emergence of an influence. The dependence of literary influence on the concepts of poetry prevailing at any one time is one of the particularly important questions which have been neglected.

But it may be that from this angle, exploring the *why* and *wherefore*, the background and the conditions of influences, a treatment of this worn-out topic could still be made fruitful. For even if we accept the various misgivings and uncertainties mentioned at the beginning of this article, this should not lead us into

[1] See e.g. René Wellek, 'The Concept of Evolution in Literary History', *Concepts of Criticism*, 1963. Harry Levin, 'Notes on Convention', *Perspectives of Criticism*, 1950 and in *Revue de Littérature Comparée XXVII* (1953), 25.

resignation and make us give up further studies in this field. Granted that in a good many cases a literary influence is difficult to diagnose and to disentangle, there nevertheless remains a large body of significant influences which are incontestable. For no one could seriously claim that Senecan drama had no influence on pre-Shakespearean tragedy, that Spenser and Milton did not influence eighteenth-century poetry, that Tennyson was not influenced by Keats or T. S. Eliot by Donne and the French symbolists. But preoccupation with the extent of these influences and their textual proof has obviously led to the neglect of the questions of 'why' and 'wherefore'.

The question *why* is not, however, appropriate to all major influences. To ask why Spenser influenced Elizabethan poetry is beside the point; but to ask why his work gained a new importance for some poets in the eighteenth century may be revealing. It is not the influences coming from the immediate vicinity which demand our special attention, but it is those influences coming from a remote source, from a past century, which require an interpretation on the lines suggested above. For a poet who is discontented with the existing fashion, and wants to create something new, looks out for models which do not come from his immediate predecessors and he may find them in the past or in types of literature outside the accepted prevalent literary tradition. He feels that what he wants to say cannot be expressed through the current language of poetry and its traditional forms. In this situation the literature of the past may furnish him with stylistic patterns or conventions which correspond to what he is aiming at.

Influences may thus function as allies, endorsing and confirming what has already been felt as a need for new means of expression. But as the model from the past originated under entirely different circumstances, corresponding to a different state of consciousness and culture, it is clear that it can act only as a stimulus. The very fact that it is used by a poet of a much later period will inevitably change its essence; it must necessarily be transformed by the subjective searching, the 'wishful thinking' of the later poet.

But influences such as these, running counter to the prevailing norms, will act as allies in yet another sense. For a poet who is born into a firmly-established tradition of generally-accepted norms will find it extremely difficult to break through these barriers, to write in a manner which may be rejected by the public and be offensive to their taste. The model from the past, the forgotten convention of an earlier literary period, may encourage him in his audacious endeavours to break loose from the fetters of existing norms. Influences of the past could thus give a licence to the poet to say things in the vein of an author long dead which when uttered independently would scarcely be acceptable.

However, influences from the past, which are thus called upon to help bring about innovations and significant turns of literary history, serve yet another end. They keep the past alive in the literature of the present, they erect bridges across the space of centuries, they bind together authors, works, and periods which are separated by a gulf of time. This emergence of past models at moments of crisis and change should warn us not to think of a literary 'revolution' in terms of a complete break with literary tradition. It may be merely a revival of even older patterns of form and style. Each new generation selects for itself a new set of models, establishes a new pedigree of 'literary ancestry', from which to draw and to learn. No literary generation ever began at point zero.

The development of English literature has never taken a straight course. Instead it has been a dynamic process, a constant encounter of conservative and progressive forces, a conflict between opposite tendencies. Influences may be signs of what is going on below the surface. Thus in the eighteenth century a great number of forces were at work to prepare the soil for the new poetry of Romanticism. No critic, however, would be able to disentangle the complex web of impulses coming from diverse corners, from social and political transformations, from new ideas raised by philosophers or scientists, from cultural trends and events inside and outside England. Statements about the exact place held by literary influences within this intricate encounter of varied forces must remain guesswork. We can at best indicate the general development to which these influences contributed in some sense or other.

With these restrictions in mind, it can be said that Spenser as well as Milton, each of them in a different manner, helped poets of the eighteenth century to free themselves from the classicist ideal, to find new means of expression and to look out for values which had been ignored by classicist poetry. This process takes on a very different character with each of the poets of this transitional period: Young, Thomson, Gray, Collins, Shenstone and Cowper. It would be beyond the scope of this essay to describe the various stages of Spenser's and Milton's influence on poets of the eighteenth century, for each poet appears to have learned something different from either Milton or Spenser, and the manner in which the influence was exerted varied in each case: there was conscious imitation as in Thomson's *Castle of Indolence*; there was the impact of versification, or syntax, or vocabulary; there was the 'grand style', the sense for the sublime as transmitted by Milton; there were new themes, new subject matter, new aspects from past ages. The various channels through which the Middle Ages (or characteristics which people then believed to be medieval) influenced literature, are well known. The revival of the folk ballads and their impact on Coleridge and Keats should be mentioned as a case of particularly complex influence, comprising not only verse form and language, but also manner of presentation and subject matter. But Spenser's *Faerie Queene* also served as a vehicle for transmitting medieval themes and colouring. A literary influence from the sixteenth century was thus intensified by an influence from the Middle Ages.

In great poets like Spenser and Milton there is a potential influence which changes from period to period, from poet to poet so that it seems impossible to predict which facet of their work will inspire successive generations. Their influence may even provoke opposite reactions. For Milton acted as a stimulus to Dryden and Pope, as well as to those poets who strove to move away from them.

Furthermore, the influence of a great poet is by no means always beneficial. T. S. Eliot's verdict on the bane of Milton's influence: 'There is more of Milton's influence in the badness of bad verse of the eighteenth century than of anybody's else: he certainly did more harm than Dryden and Pope' was slightly modified in his second essay on Milton, but even before him critics had quoted examples of Milton's harmful influence on later poets.[1] The truth is that with all powerful influences there are a great many possibilities for good and bad. And sometimes the influence of one poet on another may serve both ends, fostering certain qualities while suppressing others, exaggerating at the cost of others certain elements of style which had been previously neglected. This ambiguous quality of influences could well be studied when we look at the poetical biography of poets such as Burns, Blake, Wordsworth, Byron and Keats.

Keats is a particularly illuminating example of a poet who consciously submitted himself to the influence of other poets in order to find eventually his own manner of writing. For him influences were stepping-stones to his own maturity, phases of exploration and experiment on the road towards himself. Critics have noted the way in which he first followed and then rejected the influence of Hunt and later the influence of Milton (traceable in the two versions of *Hyperion*). For in Keats an extraordinary openness and sensitivity to the work of others was combined with a 'vigorously critical attitude to the poets who influenced him',[2] from which only Shakespeare and Spenser were excepted.

With Keats, therefore, influences can only partly be described as 'allies'. Hunt, Haydon, Wordsworth, Milton and Scott were accepted by him as temporary masters whom he left again when he had learned certain things from them, realizing at the same time that their model did not wholly suit his own purpose, and that his own gifts, his own fulfilment, lay in another direction. Influences with Keats (again excepting Shakespeare and Spenser) were something to be overcome, after their initial impulse had acted as an incentive to the evolution of his style. In poetical

[1] E.g. Oliver Elton, *A Survey of English Literature 1730–1780*, 1928, vol. I, Ch. XII; L. Binyon in *Seventeenth Century Studies*, 1938, p. 190: 'His influence on later blank verse was disastrous.'

[2] E. C. Pettet, *On the Poetry of Keats*, 1957, p. 40.

biography, influences have acted not only as 'liberators' but equally often as impediments, signalling the poet's progress but also his setbacks and deviations. For Tennyson, for instance, the influence of Keats (although only a partial influence) had a beneficial effect, his 'gradual breaking away from Keats' was, in the opinion of some critics, a loss and 'marked the decline of his poetry'.[1]

Some poets seem to have used an influence as a kind of antidote against prevailing trends and also against their own former inclinations. Byron's choice of Pope and Dryden as his new masters could be interpreted in this way. The technique he learned from them helped him to attack the vogue of romantic sentimentality and rhetorical pathos which he himself had previously cultivated, and the demand for precision of statement, coming from Pope, counterbalanced some weaknesses of his own style.

The names of Spenser, Milton and Keats must not, however, lead us to believe that it is always the major poets whose influence is far-reaching and worth studying. Substantial influences have often come from mediocre authors and works because they evidently provided what was needed at a certain time, or because their recipients projected their own wishes into these works and interpreted them accordingly. The most revealing example of this subjective striving after ideals is the influence of Macpherson's *Ossian*, in England as well as on the Continent. For the whole of Europe, including authors of considerable critical acumen, was taken in and deeply influenced by what turned out to be a fake. The intensity of the quest for new sources of inspiration had made a whole generation blind to the obvious stylistic and thematic contradictions which emerge between the vague poetic prose pieces with their rhapsodic outbursts and a genuine Gaelic heroic epic. How can we account for the enormous success of this forgery? Macpherson had absorbed the moods of his own time and had attributed them to a period fifteen hundred years earlier, with the result that everyone felt his own longings and ideals con-

---

[1] George H. Ford, *Keats and the Victorians, A Study of his Influence and Rise to Fame* (1944/1962).

firmed by the Ossian epics. As we have seen, every new intellectual movement looks for guidance and models in the literature of the past in order to find encouragement, confirmation of its own as-yet-unarticulated desires. In this case, the required model was, as it were, 'invented'.

To explore such instances of the immense influence of works which today we consider mediocre is particularly helpful in revealing the strange laws that rule the course of literary history. The enormous fascination and the unusually complex influence exercised by Seneca on the Elizabethans is a case in point,[1] urging us to ask 'Why?'. In fact each century offers examples of authors and works with a deep influence on succeeding generations, although today they are almost forgotten. The strength and the scope of an influence does not depend on quality or on aesthetic values. The 'misconceived' influence plays as important a part in literary history as the 'objective' influence (if there has ever been one).

For the full impact of a poet is rarely transmitted. Influence has often acted as an instrument of selection, reduction, and sometimes of distortion. Chaucer's influence on his followers in the fifteenth century may serve as an example. It was neither Chaucer's humour nor his humanity, neither his subtlety nor his dramatic power that lived on, but predominantly the allegorical form of the early poems with its didactic implications, and his descriptive technique. Thus the original ratio of components was altered, the balance was destroyed and the substance of Chaucer's poetry was diluted and marred.

The achievement of a major poet is often characterized by the coming together of various strands of literary tradition, the amalgamation of heterogeneous conventions and styles. Chaucer's 'originality', the liveliness, complexity and vitality of his work resulted in some measure from the fusing of French and Italian influences with native literary tradition, from his extraordinary ability to absorb, transform and integrate material of the most varied provenance. The same can be said of a major poet in our own century, T. S. Eliot, although influence, in the twentieth

[1] See my *English Tragedy before Shakespeare*, 1961.

century, means something different and works in a different way. Eliot's pronouncement: 'Surely, the great poet is, among other things, one who not merely restores a tradition which has been in abeyance, but one who in his poetry re-twines as many straying strands of tradition as possible,'[1] could also be applied to the manner in which, in good poetry, dissimilar literary influences are combined in order to be transformed into something new and original. For the critic, however, this very fusion makes it all the more difficult to disentangle the various strands within a given text. Even the 'influenced poet' himself is scarcely in a better position. Eliot, speaking of the influence of Donne and other poets, confesses: 'It is impossible for us and for anyone else ever to disentangle how much was genuine affinity, genuine appreciation and how much was just a reading into poets like Donne our own sensibility, how much was "subjective".'[2] But we may well ask whether this 'disentangling' is really necessary and would help us very much. Studies in influence should not be an end but a means. The recognition of influences, even if it cannot be proved from detailed textual analysis, helps us to characterize the work in question, to understand more fully its place within the history of literature and to appreciate its achievement in terms of literary traditions and developments.

Studies of influence will rarely yield fruitful results when they are undertaken for their own sake. They form one of several questions which we may put when we are confronted with issues of literary history, with single works or whole trends. But we ought to put the question and should not simply ignore it. It will at least sharpen our vision, make us think about the nature of relationships and affinities, about motivations and preconditions, and will also compel us to find out more about the characteristic features and elements of the work under discussion. The pursuit of influence could thus result in a new approach to the phenomenon of originality, as was aptly expressed by Anna Balakian[3]: 'One is sometimes led to wonder whether any study of influence

---

[1] *The Use of Poetry and the Use of Criticism*, 1933, p. 85.
[2] *A Garland for John Donne*, ed. Th. Spencer (1958), p. 6.
[3] In her article in *Yearbook of Comp. and Gen. Literature* 11, 1962.

is truly justified unless it succeeds in elucidating the particular qualities of the borrower, in revealing along with the influence, and almost in spite of it, what is infinitely more important: the turning point at which the writer frees himself of the influence and finds his originality.'

VIII

Literature and Money

LAURENCE LERNER

Let us begin with a famous old tale about money, that of the three young men who went in search of Death, and found a pile of gold—and so found Death. It is known to us of course as the story of *The Pardoner's Tale,* but it is older than Chaucer. The earliest known version is in one of the birthtales of Buddha, and there are several late medieval versions, always as an illustration of the evils of avarice. In *Novella* 83 of a collection, published in 1525 (*Le ciento novelle antike*) but whose material is thought to go back to the 13th century, Jesus, out walking with his disciples, sees a treasure and warns them not to take any because it will rob them of their souls—as they'll see if they watch what happens to the robbers who find it (which they do). In an *exemplum de avaricia* from a MS written at Prague in 1406, a hermit finds a treasure and runs off crying in a loud voice 'Death, death, death!' In the 15th-century play *Representazione di Sant' Antonio*, the spirit of Avarice actually appears rejoicing at the end, and a moral points out how much evil comes from this cursed she-wolf.[1] The story caught the medieval imagination, as it had caught the oriental imagination long since, and for much the same reason: it was a warning against the lure of worldly wealth.

Chaucer's version is slightly unusual, in that it does not begin with the heap of gold: so it is only on turning to other versions that we see clearly that this is the most important detail in the story. The fighting and the poisoning are consequences of the money; the quest for Death with which Chaucer begins makes a brilliant ironic setting, but the story is centrally not about boasting

---

[1] All the material in this paragraph is taken from Frederick Tupper's study of *The Pardoner's Tale* in *Sources and Analogues of Chaucer's Canterbury Tales,* ed. Bryan and Dempster, The Humanities Press, N.Y., 1958, pp. 415–438.

but about greed. This is said explicitly by the Pardoner when he explains that he always preaches on the same subject, *radix malorum est cupiditas*; and the fact that he is himself totally dominated by greed simply adds, of course, a characteristically Chaucerian irony.

The view of money conveyed by this story is overwhelmingly moral. There is no suggestion that money is an ordinary thing, needed for the continuance of everyday social life: it is a temptation and a threat, offering dreams of unearned opulence, or bringing conflict and lurid death. There is one moment in Hans Sachs' 16th-century version of the story[1] when the hermit, after fleeing the sight of the treasure, comes back, reflecting that it may be useful to the poor, but finally decides to shun it after all. This might look at first like a different attitude to wealth, but it isn't really; for even this good use suggested for it is something exceptional. Against wealth as a form of corruption is set the possibility of wealth as a way of rectifying the injustices of society: in neither case is it seen as part of normal social activity. It is there to test our moral worth: usually to corrupt, possibly to help, but always as a moral test.

There is little in common between Chaucer's tragically ironic narrative and Shakespeare's Plautine farce, *The Comedy of Errors*: so it will be all the more striking if we can find a resemblance in their view of money. What sort of society does the play depict? The opening scene makes it clear that Ephesus and Syracuse are both trading towns: their enmity sprang from unfair treatment of each others' merchants. Egeon, father of the twins, is a merchant, and so (we must presume) is Antipholus of Ephesus, who keeps a large establishment, lives in comfort, and is a friend of the Duke. Certainly he can hardly live on inherited wealth, since he arrived in Ephesus a foundling; but all we see of his life suggests a gentleman of leisure. No doubt there is good literary reason for this: Shakespeare wants us to see Ephesus through the bewildered eyes of the Syracusans, for whom the town is full of cosinage, in Fairyland where you talk with goblins, so he naturally peoples it with a sense of danger and a leisured class, not with

[1] *Der Dot im Stock* (between 1554-1556), Tupper, *op. cit.*, pp. 429-36.

sober industry. Whatever the reason, there can be no doubt of the result. We see Antipholus as master of his time whose only duty is to get home for dinner. His sister-in-law refers briefly to his meeting merchants in the mart, but she seems to think of this activity as an assertion of male independence of the home ('A man is master of his liberty') rather than as a way of earning a living. The only transaction we see him indulging in is ordering a gold chain for his wife; and the only person who handles money is the other Antipholus, who has brought it with him—and even that money is never spent, it is merely the occasion for a comic beating and a series of misunderstandings. The chain does change hands, but to the wrong Antipholus, who in a world of common-sense would not accept it, but who takes it as a sign of the magical wealth, the 'golden gifts' of Ephesus.

All mention of the practical functions of money has been carefully removed. We neither know nor care how Antipholus of Ephesus keeps his establishment going, and it is only the foils and social inferiors, like Angelo and Balthazar, who have to worry about paying their debts. Yet money is prominent in the Anti-pholus-Dromio situations, as an occasion for confusion, or as a test of good intention. The reason Angelo does not get his money for the chain is not because chains are expensive and Antipholus was extravagant, but because of the confusions of the comic plot. If we compare this with *The Pardoner's Tale* we can see that we have moved from tragedy to farce, but are still in a world unconcerned with the practical purpose of money.

What would an alternative view of money be like? It would see it not in moral but in functional terms: as something we take trouble to acquire, and spend with care and judgement. As something we earn in reasonable and variable amounts, over time, not suddenly and unexpectedly; and as something we need for everyday wants. Even the poisoned drink that the youngest rioter bought had to be paid for: as the ordinary, unpoisoned drink and bread that we buy every day.

To see this other view, as an extreme contrast, let us turn to *Middlemarch*. When Tertius Lydgate arrives in the town as an ambitious young medical practitioner, he knows it will be unwise to marry too soon. Not yet established in practice, determined to pursue his scientific researches, he has neither time nor money for domestic life: chatting to Mayor Vincy's accomplished daughter is all very well—mild flirtatious chat, laced with sexual tension but perfectly proper and (most important) non-committal. But marriage is an arrangement that changes one's way of life, and which presupposes capital and/or a regular income.

Lydgate, as we know, was caught by his own sexual susceptibility. Why did his marriage ruin his career? The obvious answer is, because his wife had neither the imaginative sympathy to share poverty with him, nor the economic sense to manage their money matters. Rosamund clearly does not understand money. When her mother is chattering to her, in a very down-to-earth way, about where to buy linen, and how to furnish a house, she remarks that Mr Vincy is not going to give any money. 'Do you think Mr. Lydgate expects it?' To this Rosamund answers: 'You cannot imagine that I should ask him, mamma. Of course he understands his own affairs' (chapter 36).

All Rosamund's education is implied in this supremely self-satisfied remark. Her bland lack of interest in Lydgate's affairs suggests feminine submission, but in a way it is feminine dominance as well: for it is this refusal to be involved with his problems that breaks Lydgate. And although Rosamund would consider it unladylike to interest herself in financial details, it would equally be unladylike not to expect the results. As George Eliot has already told us, 'There was nothing financial, still less sordid, in her previsions: she cared about what were considered refinements, and not about the money that was to pay for them' (ch. 12).

Here is one of the central insights of George Eliot's realism: that in order to be above money, you need to have it. Rosamund is a very expensive plant; and the very fact that she has been trained not to think about expense, makes her more expensive still. In both Rosamund and her brother Fred we can see this contempt for anything 'sordid', and we can see how their upbringing caused it; yet it would be quite wrong to blame Lydgate's troubles entirely on her. Just as he would not have married her if he had looked for strength of character rather than charm and accomplishment in a wife, so he would not have allowed himself to get into such difficulties if he too had not been above such sordid matters as financial calculation. These are the famous 'spots of commonness' in Lydgate's character: the fact that he did not apply to human and social matters the high qualities of mind that he showed as a scientist.

Lydgate entered into treaty for old Mrs. Bretton's house

> in an episodic way, very much as he gave orders to his tailor for every requisite of perfect dress, without any notion of being extravagant. On the contrary, he would have despised any ostentation of expense; his profession had familiarised him with all grades of poverty, and he cared much for those who suffered hardships. He would have behaved perfectly at a table where the sauce was served in a jug with the handle off, and he would have remembered nothing about a grand dinner except that a man was there who talked well. But it had never occurred to him that he should live in any other than what he would have called an ordinary way, with green glasses for hock, and excellent waiting at table (ch. 36).

How well George Eliot knew Lydgate: the perfection of his behaviour as a doctor, combined with his assumption that none of these difficulties he knew how to make allowance for would ever apply to *him*. There is a good deal more about Lydgate's preparations for marriage, all imbued with George Eliot's marvellous insight that the sensitive taste which does not calculate is in fact insensitive:

> Happening the next day to accompany a patient to Brassing, he saw a dinner-service there which struck him as so exactly the right thing that he bought it at once. It saved time to do these things just when you thought of them, and Lydgate hated ugly crockery. The dinner-service in question was expensive, but that might be in the nature of dinner-services (ch. 36).

'Lydgate hated ugly crockery': how the short, blunt sentence reveals the curtness with which he shuts out the nicely calculated less or more. And when Mrs Vincy says she hopes it won't be broken, Lydgate's reply is once more revealing: '"One must hire servants who will not break things," said Lydgate.' What it would be vulgar to inquire into is treated with the magic word 'must'. It is the same shedding of responsibility Lydgate has already shown over marriage: one must marry a wife who will make one's home gracious. Lydgate does not know about the material basis of domestic affection, he takes it for granted; so it is not surprising that he finds a wife who does the same.

There is one character in *Middlemarch* who does understand the material basis: that is Mr Farebrother, the clergyman, who understands so much. Lydgate is a little shocked to find Mr Farebrother playing cards for money; and since he usually has more insight into other people's situation than his own, realizes that Farebrother needs the money, and relies on his winnings. When—partly through Lydgate's help—Farebrother finds himself better off financially, he remarks

It's rather a strong check to one's self-complacency to find how much of one's right doing depends on not being in want of money. A man will not be tempted to say the Lord's Prayer backwards to please the devil, if he doesn't want the devil's services (ch. 63).

The details of domestic economy—details which old-fashioned readers might feel beneath their consideration—are for George Eliot the true meaning of money: something a professional man has to earn bit by bit, and a family man has to spend with care. That is what I suggest we should call the functional not the moral view of money. This terminology is, I admit, tendentious: is not George Eliot renowned as one of the most deeply moral of novelists? But though a moralist, she is also a realist: her first concern is to render the quality of social experience to show us what taking a decision is like, by making sure we understand fully what the choice is between; only then are we led to ask, what was the right decision. The traditional view of money, however, is moral at the expense of realism: the categories of social perception are themselves formed by the moral scheme. It is to emphasize this difference that I suggest a terminology by which our great novelist of moral concern is not placed among the moralists.

Yet the traditional view of money is found in *Middlemarch* too. The one story that uses a very old comic formula is that of Featherstone, the bed-ridden miser, whose greatest delight is in tormenting the relatives who hope to inherit his wealth. He uses money as a lure and a threat—as an assault on human emotions, not as a practical necessity for living. Greedy himself, he arranges and gloats over a satiric comedy in which *radix malorum est cupiditas*. And so when Featherstone is dead and the relatives gather for the reading of the will, George Eliot prints as epigraph (ch. 35) a few lines from *Le légataire universel* of Regnard, a follower of Molière, describing the discomfiture of the legacy-hunters who get nothing but *un bonsoir avec un pied de nez*. These conventional lines about the corrupting effect of greed, in a comic form that goes back through Molière to Terence and Juvenal, now commend themselves to her as appropriate for her own satire. Yet as we read the chapter, we soon discover that it is not traditional satire after all.

> Poor Mrs. Cranch being half moved with the consolation of getting any hundreds at all without working for them, and half aware that her share was scanty; whereas Mrs. Waule's mind was entirely flooded with the sense of being an own sister and getting little, while somebody else was to have much (ch. 35).

The situation is that of Regnard or Juvenal; but the treatment is that of George Eliot. These women have families and comprehensions of their own: they lack the sharpness (and also the simplicity) of a Voltore or a Tartuffe.

This mingling of convention and realism is seen perfectly in the story of Fred Vincy and Stone Court, old Featherstone's home. Fred had always hoped, and sometimes thought, that the property would be left to him; and is naturally disappointed when it isn't. But in the end Fred, because he is the hero and has come through his trials successfully, does get the property, and there lives happily with wife and children. To tell the story in summary like this is to make it sound like a fairytale; but how different when we look at what actually happens. For Fred does not earn Stone Court by passing magic tests in the manner of the youngest son who helps the fairy disguised as an old woman, or of Bassanio, the spend-thrift who knows how to moralize and choose the leaden casket while he makes a speech against money. Fred's triumph lies in accepting his disappointment and living through its consequences. Because he has lost his expectations he has to work; he still has the same careless character, and he has to learn to do small un-comfortable things, like giving up billiards and learning to write legibly, not large symbolic things like making speeches or choos-ing caskets. Fred gets a real, not a symbolic Stone Court: and he gets it because he has shown himself competent to manage it. His response to his disappointment is not the fine moral gesture of learning to despise riches, but the practical measure of learning to work instead of living in hopes.

I have so far discussed money in terms of its effects on men's lives, that is, in functional terms; but we can add a word on the form of its existence as object. For here too there is a clear contrast between the moral and the functional treatment. In the medieval stories money is gold coins, glinting with temptation and chinking the tune of corruption. Chaucer's rogues found

> Of floryns fyne of goldey-coyned rounde
> Wel ny an eighte busshels, as hem thoughte.[1]

Hans Sachs' hermit saw the treasure in an old tree-stump, and ran away from it. Wealth in this tale is a physical object. But for Lydgate, money is represented by those abstractions that the economy finds convenient: banknotes, bills and cheques. In order to find that he is in difficulties, he does not count coins, he per-forms calculations. The only moment in *Middlemarch* at which money takes on a vivid physical existence is when old Featherstone is dying, and wants Mary to burn a will for him. As he grows

[1] *The Pardoner's Tale, Canterbury Tales* C 770-1 (Skeat's text: Oxford, 1912).

desperate at her refusal he opens the tin box in which he keeps his money, and offers it all to her, the notes and the gold.

> Mary, standing by the fire, saw its red light falling on the old man, propped up on his pillows and bed-rest, with his bony hand holding out the key, and the money lying on the quilt before him. She never forgot that vision of a man wanting to do as he liked at the last (ch. 33).

Here the novel has taken on a different kind of power from usual —something more traditional and less realistic, more in terms of vivid symbolic moments and less of the slow pressure of actuality; and it is wholly appropriate that at this moment we *see* money as nowhere else in the book.

Georg Simmel points out, in his essay on Secrecy,[1] that money enables transactions to be carried on in 'otherwise unattainable secrecy'. Three characteristics of money make this possible: its compressibility ('which permits one to make somebody rich by slipping a cheque into his hand without anybody's noticing it'), its abstractness, and its effect-at-a-distance. This possibility is a sign of the large impersonal group. The literary point I have been making confirms Simmel's view: in our society, the more important the money, the more abstract its form. The child spending his pocket money feels the coins in his hand, and knows by physical contact how much he has. Wages come in the somehow less tangible form of banknotes, that were once mere promises, like cheques, and have now come to seem to us like real money as they have grown less important. It is cheques that really matter now, or share certificates, or other statements of transactions that take place only through ledgers or computers. Gold coins chink only in antique shops, where they are 'paid for' with paper.

George Eliot is not the only novelist (though she is perhaps the most brilliant) to offer us the functional treatment of money: indeed, it could be claimed that every great 19th-century novelist uses it, since they are all analysts of the workings of their society. For a brief example, I turn to Trollope.

[1] *The Sociology of Georg Simmel*, ed. K. H. Wolff (New York, 1950), p. 335.

Trollope's interest in the traditional landed aristocracy is respectful but shrewd: he is aware that it is infiltrated from commerce and the professions, and concerned to study the response. He is concerned too with the further infiltration of foreigners into commerce and finance. His picture, as is natural in a writer more voluminous than subtle, is detailed and elaborate. He is concerned with the difference between the great families, often active in politics, wealthy and needing even more wealth, and the squirearchy, more conservative, more detached from the centre of power, and to Trollope's mind more truly representative of traditional English virtue. He is concerned too with the upstarts and the immigrants, and how English society adjusts itself to receive them. His finest study of this situation—perhaps his finest novel— is *The Way We Live Now*, the story of the rise and fall of the Jewish financier Melmotte. Trollope does not care for Melmotte: he shows him as dishonest, blustering, and coarse, and he considers his success a symptom of the decline of English society—hence the novel's title. Yet the book is not a simple piece of xenophobia. Not only is Trollope careful to have a good Jewish financier to contrast with the corrupt ones; he keeps his most savage satire for the young English noblemen who do nothing except drink, hunt, gamble, and quarrel with their fathers, and who are perfectly prepared to use Melmotte for their own convenience while continuing to despise him.

What we have here is a hierarchical society which is having to change: the landed interest can only survive if it comes to terms with the moneyed interest. Of course this has always happened in English society: Pitt actually suggested that every man with a thousand a year should be raised to the peerage.[1] So when Plantaganet Palliser, rising politician and heir to a dukedom, marries Glencora for her vast wealth, he is only doing what Dukes and landed politicians have always done. But because the process is now happening faster, it is more noticeable: the traditional classes have no longer time to absorb the new and make them like themselves. Trollope has a very simple way of showing this

[1] Cited by Gordon Ray in *Thackeray: The Age of Wisdom* (1958), p. 26.

change: what ought not to be bought or sold can now be had for money.[1]

The squirearchy's attitude to money is revealed in *The Way We Live Now* by that heart-of-oak Englishman Roger Carbury. He has a Roman Catholic priest staying with him, whom he describes as follows:

> Certainly he is a gentleman. He took his degree at Oxford, and then became what we call a pervert, and what I suppose they call a convert. He has not got a shilling in the world beyond what they pay him as a priest, which I take it amounts to about as much as the wages of a day labourer. He told me the other day that he was absolutely forced to buy second-hand clothes (ch. 15).

Why does the priest's lack of money not make him socially unacceptable? Because it is not a sign of class distinction. There is a distinction in Roger's mind between a gentleman and an inferior that does not appear to depend on money. Of course all such distinctions *are* based on property: a gentleman is someone who belongs to the possessing class. But on the individual level, property is expendable: Father Barham is a gentleman because he has the attributes of his class—manners, speech, interests. No doubt this makes him acceptable because it is seen as a kind of guarantee that he will not threaten the class interest. Roger Carbury is perfectly prepared to make friends with a poor priest; whereas to make friends with a poor labourer would have been socially subversive.

Into this world, where there are things money can't buy, and lack of money can't forfeit, comes Melmotte and buys everything. He simply tramples the unwritten rules and uses his vast wealth to buy what ought not to be for sale, but that a corrupt aristocracy is all too willing to sell.

---

[1] Not that Trollope's fiction is all that far from contemporary fact. There seems to be no satiric intention behind such a deadpan statement as 'The Cost of a Modern Belle', in *The Family Friend*. Sept. 1858: quoted in J. A. Banks, *Prosperity and Parenthood* (1954), p. 97.

The ball was opened by a quadrille in which Lord Buntingford, the eldest son of the Duchess, stood up with Marie. Various arrangements had been made, and this among them. We may say that it had been a part of the bargain. . . .

'Of course they are vulgar,' the Duchess had said, 'so much so as to be no longer distasteful because of the absurdity of the thing. I dare say he hasn't been very honest. When men make so much money, I don't know how they can have been honest. Of course it's done for a purpose. It's all very well saying that it isn't right, but what are we to do about Alfred's children? Miles is to have £500 a year. . . .

'Of course they expect something in return; do dance with the girl once.' Lord Buntingford disapproved—mildly, and did as his mother asked him (*ibid.* ch. 4).

For a popular Victorian novelist, Trollope can be remarkably cynical; and the main effect of *The Way We Live Now*, for all its sentimentality and leisurely pace, is of a cynical bluntness. There are even blunter passages than this one, but this is fierce enough. If the Duchess had been asked what 'vulgar' meant, she would no doubt have said it meant doing anything for money, just what she is doing. All that is left of her breeding is the habit of despising those who do openly what she barely conceals. English society, Trollope seems to be saying, consists of those who can make money, and use it to buy rank, and those who have rank, and sell it for money.

If space permitted I would here like to discuss a number of other novelists—for instance, Balzac and Dickens. Balzac shows the difference between Paris and the provinces in terms of their contrasting conceptions of money. Like Trollope he treats money functionally but; in Dickens, that great throwback to earlier literary traditions, the moral view, is predominant as in the Golden Dustman and his heap of dirt (which equals money!); though there is a more realistic anti-Dickens who is occasionally well aware of its everyday functions.[1]

But to concentrate on the nineteenth-century novel may seem

[1] The books most relevant to such a discussion would be *Illusions Perdues, Le Père Goriot, Dombey and Son* and *Our Mutual Friend.*

to be weighing things unfairly in favour of the functional view: so I ought to conclude by showing briefly what sort of literary power the moral treatment was capable of. Perhaps its finest expression is *Volpone*.

The theme here is of course traditional. Legacy hunters were a common object of satire in ancient literature, and we have seen how even George Eliot touched on the theme. Jonson's profoundly traditional originality lies in the verbal richness with which he handles the theme of riches and the fact of gold. The morning hymn to gold which opens the play is a parody of a creation hymn, in which the literal gold of the coins is endowed with the quickening power of the metaphoric gold of sunlight:

> Hail the world's soul, and mine . . .
> That lying here among my other hoards,
> Shew'st like a flame by night, or like the day
> Struck out of chaos, when all darkness fled
> Unto the centre (i, i, 3 ff.)

This is parody taken to the point of greatness: it contains the very abilities whose abuse it is satirizing. Volpone's moral error is based on a misuse of metaphor; but poetry like this is impossible unless we take metaphor seriously.

The resulting tension reproduces perfectly Jonson's ambivalent attitude to the rogues he both identifies with and condemns. Even in the harsher, sourer poetry of Mosca—

>   and, gentle sir,
> When do you come to swim in golden lard
> Up to the arms in honey, that your chin
> Is borne up stiff with fatness of the flood (i. iii. 69 ff.)

we cannot fail to be involved as well as disgusted (as is Mosca: and we share his complexity and add the irony of our distance from him).

The money which yields such brilliant poetry in *Volpone* is never earned; it is acquired through a battle of wits among the parasites. Volpone himself is very proud of the way he has got rich

> I glory
> More in the cunning purchase of my wealth,
> Than in the glad possession, since I gain
> No common way; I use no trade, no venture;
> I wound no earth with plough-shares, fat no beasts,
> To feed the shambles; have no mills for iron,
> Oil, corn, or men, to grind them into powder:
> I blow no subtle glass, expose no ships
> To threat'nings of the furrow-faced sea;
> I turn no monies in the public bank,
> Nor usure private (i, i. 30 ff.)

Volpone is an artist, something like Jonson himself: thinking up his schemes shows the same talent that went to writing the play he is in, and this identification of author and rogue produces much of the complexity of our involvement in the play. But for our present discussion, what is even more interesting is Volpone's dismissal of all other ways of acquiring money. Simple-minded Marxist critics have seen Volpone here (and Jonson too) as a critic of capitalism, and certainly the reference to

> mills for iron,
> Oil, corn, *or men*, to grind them into powder

is a marvellously economical attack on exploitation, just as *turning monies in the public bank* makes financial dealings sound vaguely distasteful. But Volpone is not a social critic, he is a parasite: his distaste for capitalism does not imply a preference for any other form of economic organisation.

> I wound no earth with ploughshares, fat no beasts
> To feed the shambles.

Agriculture is made to sound as distasteful as usury: Volpone is not against capitalism, he is against productive work.

Jonson never invites us to think about ordinary uses of money, commercial, domestic or industrial, and it is hard to see how, in his almost total reliance on metaphor for his effects, he could have. *Volpone* (this is its greatness) makes no attempt to turn into a realistic novel; and instead of offering us the functional view of money it treats money as a fetish.

Jonson's creative fetishism develops a satire on the corruption of money that can lead us, in conclusion, to a brief comparison with the most famous modern doctrine of the fetishism of money: for Marx illustrates his doctrine by quoting not (as it happens) Jonson, but a satiric passage in very much the same tradition by his great contemporary. It is now necessary to commit the rash act of trying to summarize the Marxist view of money.

Money is the alienated ability of mankind: 'that which I am unable to do as a man, I am able to do by means of money . . . Money transforms the real essential powers of man and nature into what are merely abstract conceits and therefore imperfections— into tormenting chimeras' (*Economic and Philosophical Manuscripts of 1844*). This process of abstraction produces the fetishism of commodities: the investing of objects with qualities that properly belong only to human activity and human relationships. 'Money is thus the general overturning of individualities which turns them into their contrary and adds contradictory attributes to their attributes.' Since money is the form under which commodities can be made to increase in value, capitalism must use money; and that means in turn that capitalism will lead to the fetishism of commodities, since money is the form in which the exchange-value of commodities most clearly supersedes their use-value.

When Marx attacks alienation in economic life, and fetishism in our attitudes to commodities, what he points to is the loss of the total human meaning of a situation, and money is the perfect symbol of this, since it reduces the actuality and variety of social life to the uniformity represented by price. Price ignores all particulars of a situation except those that can be stated in terms of money, i.e. of an abstraction.

Abstractions surround us everywhere. Science is not possible without the abstractions of mathematics; discussion is not possible without abstract nouns; and complex economic life may not be possible without money. Abstractions need not always be tormenting chimeras: they may be the only way of retaining control over complex systems. Yet equally we know that there are those who desire money for its own sake only, or who use abstract nouns without any awareness of what, in terms of experience, they are really talking about. We need therefore to distinguish between alienation as an inevitable process resulting from complexity, and alienation as fetishism, that is, as the distortion of values that results when a miser hoards money, the Dodson sisters hoard linen, or a philosopher (Marxist or otherwise) plays with abstract nouns that have lost real meaning. It is precisely this distinction that Marx doesn't seem to me to draw adequately; perhaps to draw it fully we need not the economist or the philosopher, but the novelist or poet.

And Marx, as if admitting this (for he was a man of wide and deep culture), quotes Shakespeare, illustrating his theory of the power of money in bourgeois society from *Timon of Athens*

> ... Why, this
> Will lug your priests and servants from your sides,
> Pluck stout men's pillows from below their heads:
> This yellow slave
> Will knit and break religions, bless the accursed;
> Make the hoar leprosy adored, place thieves
> And give them title, knee and approbation
> With senators on the bench (IV. iii. 31 ff.)

Shakespeare, says Marx, 'excellently depicts the real nature of money.' Well, what he does depict is how money turns everything topsy-turvy, how it makes 'black white, foul fair', how it turns thieves into senators. But if money overturns order and degree, what set them up in the first place? How did the senators get on the bench? If money will 'lug our priests and servants from our sides', does that mean they weren't paid in the first place? We can see that for Shakespeare money is not the mechanism that keeps society functioning, it is what causes malfunctioning. Senators and servants have their rightful places by nature, and are displaced by gold.

Now of one thing we can be certain: that this is not a description of the power of money in bourgeois society. If we have to find a social analogy for this, it would be the intrusion of money into a subsistence economy. What we have in Shakespeare is a pure version of the moral view of money. Timon's speech is wholly traditional, and has nothing to do with capitalism.

I believe that Marx's mistake, in quoting this passage, is crucial. I believe, that is, that he was not simply swept away by his enthusiasm for Shakespeare into quoting a speech that does not really illustrate his point; but that the speech partly does illustrate the point, for the point is confused. Marx is himself hovering, in the Manuscripts, between a moral and a functional view of money. He shows very interestingly, in *Capital*, that money is part of the ideological language that distorts our perception of social realities, for it makes it seem as if the capitalist has some other source of wealth than the expropriation of unpaid labour.[1] Even if this is true—even if money helps us to mis-describe social reality—that is not all it does. If production were treated as production by freely associated men, consciously regulated in accordance with a settled plan (as will happen in Marx's socialist society), something like money would no doubt still be used for convenience. I don't think Marx distinguishes, and I am quite sure most contemporary Marxists don't distinguish, between such necessary neutral abstractions, and those that ideology uses to distort social reality. It is gratifying to be able to suggest that a literary distinction can help us to criticize a social theory.

[1] See especially *Capital*, Vol. I, Part I, ch. 1, para. 4 ('The Fetishism of Commodities and the Secret Thereof') and ch. 3 ('Money, or the Circulation of Commodities').